HOW TO RESOLVE CONFLICT IN THE WORKPLACE

To Mum and Dad with love

How to Resolve Conflict in the Workplace

Hoda Lacey

Gower

Published by
Gower Publishing Limited
Gower House
Croft Road
Aldershot
Hampshire GU11 3HR
England

Gower
131 Main Street
Burlington
Vermont 05401
USA

Hoda Lacey has asserted her right under the Copyright, Designs and Patents Act 1988 to be identified as the author of this work.

British Library Cataloguing in Publication Data

Lacy, Hoda
    How to resolve conflict in the workplace
    1. Conflict management   2. Personnel management
    I. Title
    658.4'053

ISBN 0 566 08073 7

Library of Congress Cataloging-in-Publication Data

Lacey, Hoda
    How to resolve conflict in the workplace / Hoda Lacey
        p. cm.
    Includes bibliographical reference and index.
    ISBN 0-566-08073-7 (hardback)
        1. Conflict management.   2. Dispute resolution (Law).
    3. Organizational behavior.   4. Psychology, Industrial.
    5. Supervision of employees.   I. Title.
    HD42 .L33 2000
    658.4'053- -dc21

                                                    00-021273

Typeset in 11/12pt Palatino by Acorn Bookwork, Salisbury
and printed in Great Britain at the University Press, Cambridge.

Contents

List of figures and tables

Figures

Tables

Preface

In conflict, be fair and generous.

(Lao-Tzu, 604–531 BC, Chinese philosopher)

This book is for both managers and those they manage. It is for both individuals and teams.

Conflict is neither good nor bad, it is simply a fact of life. How we deal with it is what matters. Without conflicting opinions, there would be no impetus to change, no progress, no onward movement. But we can express these opinions in a positive fashion or in a negative fashion. Resolving conflict is not avoiding or suppressing conflict. It is using the conflict and turning it round so that we derive benefit from it, and grasping the opportunity to move on.

Managing conflict in the workplace is an essential skill. The chances are that if you manage staff, not only will you come into conflict with some of them but you will also be called upon to resolve conflicts between them at some point. That is why identifying and minimizing interpersonal conflict is recognized by the Management Charter Initiative as one of its National Vocational Qualification (NVQ) Occupational Standards for Managers.

In addition, government guidelines on reducing stress at work, published by the Health and Safety Executive (HSE, 1995), specifically suggests training employees in interpersonal skills and setting up systems for dealing with conflict and bullying in the workplace. Both of these are effective tools in reducing stress in the workplace which a recent Confederation of British Industry (CBI) survey claims costs taxpayers and industry an estimated £7 billion a year (IPD, 1998).

There is a more open admission of conflict in the workplace these days. My work as a management and training development consultant brings me face to face with conflict on a regular basis. I see its effect on morale, on team behaviour, on motivation, on productivity and, ultimately, on profit.

Daniel Dana, of the Mediation Training Institute International believes that unmanaged employee conflict is the largest reducible cost in organizations today and probably the least recognized.

Many managers tell me that if they did not have to spend so much time solving problems, they would have more time to actually manage. I often ask participants on my courses to estimate how much of their time is spent on conflicts. The answers range from 25 per cent to 60 per cent! Valuable time that could be spent being more productive and creative.

I have seen good employees leave organizations because they could not handle the conflict. I have seen top management turn a blind eye, denying that such problems exist within their organization, until conflict blows up into a serious confrontation. They hope that by ignoring conflict for long enough, it will resolve itself. Unfortunately, conflict does not simply disappear. It may go underground for a while but it will resurface with a vengeance when we are least expecting it.

You have probably used one or more of the tools of conflict resolution yourself in the past. You may have known what to do intuitively and may not have realized that it is a skill that can be learned. You may assume that people should be adult enough to resolve their own problems, that many of the approaches are just 'common sense', but we are not taught social or interpersonal skills at school, nor is it part of basic 'on the job' training.

This book offers you a toolkit of skills and some help in selecting the appropriate tool for the level of conflict with which you are involved. You may be skilled in one aspect but not another. The danger is that if you are skilled in using a hammer, then every problem will probably look like a nail! If an approach has worked in the past, we tend to make the problem adapt to our solution next time.

Underlying the philosophy of conflict resolution is a belief that 'together we can work this out' and taking responsibility for ourselves. If we were more able to adopt this mindset, and were prepared for open dialogue with our peers and bosses, there would be less need for official channels for grievances and less time and money spent on industrial tribunals.

This necessitates a willingness to become more co-operative, to adopt a win/win outlook and to be the one to take the first step towards resolving a conflict – even if you think the other person is at fault! And this is where conflict resolution training comes in. We are often prepared to accept apologies or let bygones be bygones so long as someone else takes the first step! No one said resolving conflict is easy.

You may have heard the adage 'If you always do what you've always done, you'll always get what you've always got'. But this applies only if we assume that circumstances remain stable and static. In a changing world, we need to adapt our behavioural repertoire to give ourselves more choices. In the past you may have been used to dealing with conflict in a certain way, and you were prepared for a particular outcome. Suddenly, you find that your old tactics are no longer working. You are doing the same thing but you are not achieving the same results. Other people and circumstances have moved on. Employees may have become more aware of their rights, more empowered, less cowed by authority. This is a new world of business and you must learn a new set of skills to go with it.

This phenomenon was most poignantly seen after the tragic death of Diana, Princess of Wales, in 1997. The royal family reacted in the way it always had. It followed tradition and behaved in the way it had always behaved. But it was dealing with a new public expectation here and neither they, nor their advisers, were able to adjust quickly enough. Anger and resentment started to mount among the people, as new behaviours and new interactions were demanded. Luckily, the Palace responded just in time and the crisis was averted.

This episode may serve as a management lesson for all of us. If you do not adapt and change your management style you are in peril.

This book is based on many of the teachings of neuro-linguistic programming (NLP), however, you do not need to be familiar with these to benefit from reading it. There are many excellent works on the market for those whose appetite is whetted by my references to NLP in *How to Resolve Conflict in the Workplace*, and some of these are listed in Appendix II.

I am often asked to describe what exactly NLP is and why so many people enthuse about it and talk about its life-changing qualities. I liken NLP to a fine wine. You can describe its clarity and colour, its nose, age, fruit and depth, and its bouquet, body, tannin and acid, but until you taste it for yourself you cannot do justice to its quality, finesse, elegance and breed.

Neuro-linguistic programming is a study of how we make up our own worlds – how we learn, how we communicate, how we think, how language affects our thoughts and experiences and how we influence people – in other words, human interaction. It has been used by therapists, communicators, managers, sales-people, athletes and performers – and by thousands of ordinary people wanting to improve themselves, their outlooks, their rela-tionships with each other and their lives. Neuro-linguistic pro-gramming, quite simply, works to reach the parts other studies cannot reach.

The book is in three Parts. Part I sets the scene, Part II presents the seven skills of conflict resolution, and the final Part provides some practical tools for resolving conflict.

Some readers may be tempted to jump straight to the last Part without working through the earlier text first, particularly if you have already undertaken some personal development work and are familiar with some of the relevant theory. But there is no point in putting the icing before the cake. The practicalities will not work unless the mindset underneath is solid. Consider this your opportunity to revise your knowledge and carry out a per-sonal inventory. We often have so much theoretical information stored in our personal databanks that we forget to draw on it when needed.

This book will:

- improve your conflict-resolving skills by giving you more tools to use;
- make you aware of what you are doing well so you can build on that;
- identify your personal Achilles' heel and inappropriate responses;
- give you an understanding of why you behave as you do;
- offer you solid practical conflict-resolving strategies.

But *How to Resolve Conflict in the Workplace* will not do these on its own. Resolving conflict is not achievable by just reading a book but it will help you to acquire a new conflict-resolving *para-digm* and a determination to put your principles into practice on every possible occasion.

I suggest you buy yourself a notebook in which to record your responses to the exercises in this book and to make notes of any conflicts you encounter over the next few weeks. Keeping a record of your emotions and interactions, both negative and positive, will raise your personal awareness and speed your personal development in all areas, not just in conflicts.

A final point. *How to Resolve Conflict in the Workplace* is based on Western values, attitudes and beliefs. If your work brings you into contact with other cultures, such as those of the Middle or Far East, you will need to research these cultures and adapt your conflict resolution skills accordingly.

Managing conflict requires examining our:

Behaviour	**Awareness**
Effectiveness	**Willingness**
Commitment	**Attitude**
Objectivity	**Responsibility**
Manner	**Energy**
Empathy	

Becoming aware is very often all that is required to start the change process. By reading this far, you are already on the right track.

Why have I written this book?

Conflict has been all around me since I first became consciously aware. I grew up in the Middle East of mixed parentage, culture and religion. Since starting my working life, I have observed the impact of conflicts at work and the toll it takes on people.

I discovered that the source of conflict is often within us. This makes us intensely uncomfortable and therefore we blame everything and everyone around us. It is always 'their fault'.

This is not to say that unreasonable or difficult people do not exist. They do. What you need to remember, though, is that *they* think *you* are the problem!

While grappling with this issue, fate brought me into contact with the teachings of the Conflict Resolution Network in Australia, a network of people with a common commitment to conflict resolution, co-operative communication strategies and related skills.

The Conflict Resolution Network (CRN) was founded by the United Nations of Australia in 1986. The material they created was Australia's contribution to the United Nations Year of Peace.

The material in the CRN course has been tried, tested and refined over ten years. It is based on the book *Everyone Can Win* by Helena Cornelius and Shoshana Faire (Cornelius and Faire, 1989) and the *12 Skills* training manual which accompanies it.

One of the most generous things that the CRN gave the world was free access to their materials, which can be photocopied and used in training courses as long as the source is clearly acknowledged in writing.

I have a great deal of interest in conflict in the corporate world and my work has brought me into touch with many different people and organizations. I have observed the same issues, emotions and reactions over and over again. I *know* that this programme works to change the underlying thought processes and thus to bring about real and lasting conflict resolution.

While this book uses much of the original '12-skills' outline, I have brought in material from many other sources that I have found inspirational and which dovetail with the original concept. Some of these you will agree with and others will sit less comfortably with you. Either way, I hope they will provoke some response. My dream for the book is that readers, whether they agree or disagree with the contents, will use it as a launching pad for their own ideas. I hope everyone who reads it will take the concepts, adapt and develop them further and then pass the message on.

Acknowledgements

First, my many thanks to Helena Cornelius of Conflict Resolution Network for her incredible generosity and guidance.

Thanks are also due to John Ryder for gifting me with Conflict Resolution (UK); Chris Markiewicz and Frieda Stanbury for their inspiration and support; Malcolm Stern at Gower for his trust and patience; Dr Peter Critten and my POD Action Learning Set at Middlesex University who gave me the confidence to tackle this project; the many participants on my courses who have taught me more than they will ever know; the wonderful books I have read; the talented trainers I have been privileged to work with and, most important, to the Ramzis, the Freebairns and Gordon.

In common with many training consultants, I often seem to acquire knowledge by a process of osmosis. I have also evolved some existing concepts to adapt to my own 'map of the world'. I have striven to name all my sources and if I have not attributed an idea or model then it is because I genuinely do not know the source.

Abbreviations

ANLP	Association of Neuro-Linguistic Programming
CBI	Confederation of British Industry
CEDR	Centre for Dispute Resolution
CRN	Conflict Resolution Network
HSE	Health and Safety Executive
IPD	Institute of Personnel and Development
IQ	intelligence quotient
IT	information technology
NLP	neuro-linguistic programming
NVQ	National Vocational Qualification
OC	organizational culture
TA	transactional analysis

Part I

The nature of conflict

1

Learning and unlearning

We shape clay into a pot, but it is the emptiness inside which holds whatever we want.

(Lao-Tzu, 604–531 BC, Chinese philosopher)

Learning and our behaviour are inextricably linked. Once we realize that much of our thoughts and behaviour is based on what we have learnt so far in life, it becomes clear that what has been learned can be unlearned. We can erase the old tapes and record new responses over them. Conflict resolution involves unlearning old reactions and replacing them with healthier and more appropriate responses.

This is a practical skills book. To become adept at resolving conflict, you need to learn new attitudes, behaviour and skills. Doing so requires willingness, commitment and perseverance.

Learning preparation

Exercise

Ask yourself the following questions and make a note of your answers:

1. What do you want from this book? What do you hope to improve? What you hope to achieve from this book may well be

3

different from another reader. You need to identify your own outcomes. Once you have done that, your unconscious mind will be put into a state of alertness and will identify specific areas of interest, and make connections you may not other-wise have made, thus speeding up your learning process.

2. What concerns do you have at present regarding your ability to handle conflict? Do you have any niggling thoughts pre-venting you from reaching your outcomes? For example, do you believe that we are born with fixed personalities and we just have to live with ourselves as we are? Or do you believe that conflict will always exist and one person cannot make a difference? Perhaps you are thinking: 'If conflict resolution works, why hasn't it worked in Northern Ireland, or Kosovo or (any other place)?'

When resolving conflict, you will often be pushed to the limit and occasionally may lose your self-control. Do not worry, even expert mediators have to take time out to rethink strategies during particularly heated conflicts.

A good way to start is to think of a past conflict and spend some time reflecting on the attitudes and behaviour you and the other party displayed and try to extract some learning from it.

Read through this section first. Then choose a place where you can be comfortable, quiet and uninterrupted. Have a notebook and pen by your side. I will ask you to review a conflict with which you were involved. Immerse yourself fully in whichever conflict comes to mind.

Then write down your observations in a notebook. This is important. Do not be tempted to skip it! Writing things down is not like thinking them over or 'mentally writing'. Reread what you have written before moving on to the next section.

Exercise

Think of a recent conflict in which you were an active party. It does not matter whether the conflict is old or recent, but that it made an impact on you. Choose an incident in which you had a face-to-face encounter with the other party(ies). Take a few moments to fully recollect.

Next, observe your own interaction with the other party(ies). It may be useful to imagine yourself as a 'fly on the wall', an objective third party. What were you saying and doing? What were you hearing? What were you feeling? What body language were you and the other party(ies) using?

Where did the incident take place? Was there anyone else present? Were you seated or standing? Was there any background noise? What time of day was it? Try to build up a picture of everything that happened – a rich picture of the incident. The more details you remember, the more you will benefit from the reflection.

Now pay attention to the here and now. What conclusions have you drawn from that conflict? Are you making any generalizations about your own behaviour in a conflict? Or that of others? For example:

- 'I can't help losing my temper when...'
- 'I'm no good at standing up for myself when...'
- 'People always take advantage of my good nature...'

If you could go back to that incident again, what would you do differently? If a similar incident were to happen again, how would these thoughts help or hinder your conflict-resolving skills?

Reinforcing faulty learning

In today's hectic environment, we rarely have the time for reflection and contemplation. Many people will find that they are reinforcing their behaviour in the manner depicted in Figure 1.1.

Let us look at an example of how this would work in practice:

1. *Having an experience.* As a new and relatively raw recruit to an office, you are up-braided publicly by your boss in an aggressive manner. You are so upset that your throat constricts, you start to shake and are unable to defend yourself.
2. *Generalizing/drawing faulty conclusions.* This experience so influences you that you tell yourself that all bosses are aggressive and you cannot stand up to authority.
3. *Allowing the above to influence your mindset/behaviour.* This belief may affect you in different ways, for example:
   (a) You may avoid all bosses and authority figures completely, communicating only in writing to avoid the emotional reaction. This further inflames the situation as the bosses then see you as a 'wimp'.

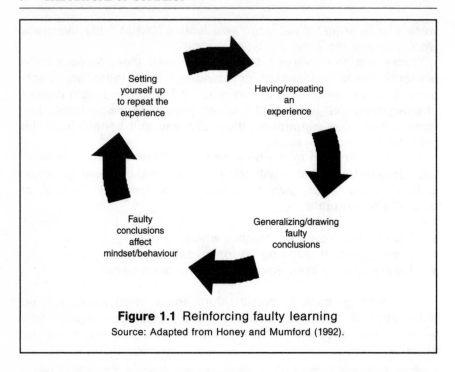

Figure 1.1 Reinforcing faulty learning
Source: Adapted from Honey and Mumford (1992).

(b) You may overcompensate for your perceived inability to defend your own position by approaching your boss in an aggressive and uncooperative manner before your boss does so to you.

(c) You may treat your own subordinates in the same way when you are in a higher position, treating them in exactly the same manner since you believe that is how bosses treat their staff.

4. *Setting yourself up to repeat the experience.* Now you can see how this mindset motivates your behaviour and how you are much more likely to provoke conflict yourself.

5. *Having an(other) experience.* This now becomes a self-fulfilling prophecy and the next experience you have reinforces the faulty mindset and so on. Your subjective experience becomes a reality for you. You do not even see the connection between your experiences and your mindset.

It is the easiest thing in the world to generalize from one experience. In fact, our brains are set up to generalize in order to help us learn. For example, if we burn ourselves on a stove as children, we generalize that we should avoid touching something very hot in order not to repeat the pain. However, as we grow older, we become, or should become, more discriminating. One way to do so is through a process of reflection.

How often do you reflect on your experiences? I mean *really* reflect, not just play them back in your mind over and over again, concentrating on what you did badly and making yourself feel even worse. Reflection requires both time and skill. Today we are so rushed that we tend to live from minute to minute and, once an experience is over, we may shrug our shoulders and decide to put it behind us. We may even think that we have learned from it. But unless we reflect on the matter and consciously extract the learning, we will set ourselves up to repeat that faulty learning pattern.

The following list is a model for structured reflection (adapted from Johns, 1995). While it is useful to have someone talk you through the experience, you can do this on your own. After a short while, reflecting will become an *unconscious skill*.

Exercise

Write a description of the experience in question. Include as many details as you can to build a full picture. Pay particular attention to words or feelings that float into your consciousness and write them down. Take a pen and highlight the main issues. Reflect on how the situation initially arose.

- Who initiated it, myself or the other party(ies)?
- What were my needs? What were the other party(ies) needs?
- Did the situation get out of control? If so, what was the trigger?
- What was I feeling at the time?
- How was the other party(ies) feeling? What leads me to believe that?
- What was I thinking at the time?
- What was the other party(ies) thinking? What leads me to believe that?
- What external factors influenced my thoughts and behaviour?
- What previous experiences influenced my thoughts and behaviour?
- What are the consequences of my actions?
- Do I need to take any further action to resolve any misunderstandings?
- With hindsight, could I have dealt better with the situation? How?

- What might have been the consequences of handling it differently?
- How am I feeling now about the situation?
- What have I learnt from it?
- Has this changed my way of thinking?

This is an extract from a reflection produced at one of my workshops (the participant's permission has been given):

> With hindsight, of course, I could have dealt better with the situation. I was taken by surprise and reacted defensively. Also my professional pride was involved and that made me even more heavy-handed. If I had taken the time to listen to what she was saying, and to see how it appeared to her I could have simply explained my motives, apologized if I appeared to have displayed preferential treatment and sorted the matter out there and then. In the event, I was so angry I escalated the matter and consequently two other people became unnecessarily involved.
>
> I don't think I would react in this way again. I feel embarrassed over my behaviour, it was petty and immature and I see that now. But I have learnt from it. I realize that it was guilt and anxiety about the consequences that caused my defensive reaction. To be honest, I don't know exactly what I would do if the situation happened again but I hope I wouldn't react in the same way.

Early programming

Our values and beliefs, our behaviour and perceptions, the very people we are today are a result of both inherited tendencies (nature) and external influences, for example how we were raised (nurture). Nurture includes physical care (warmth, food, healthy environment), emotional care (unconditional love, support and a caring environment) and intellectual care (mental stimulation/education) (Figure 1.2).

Babies are not born with low self-esteem or defeatist attitudes. With very few exceptions, they are not born aggressive, rude or disruptive. These are qualities instilled in them at some point during their upbringing.

Some of our behaviours are useful and serve our purposes

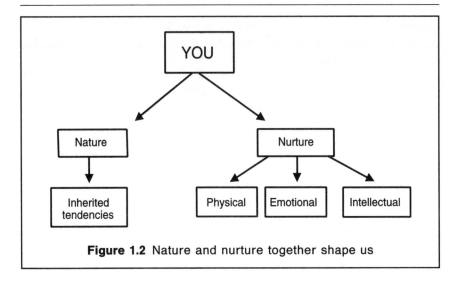

Figure 1.2 Nature and nurture together shape us

while other behaviours hinder our progress and adversely influence the way we interact with others.

For example:

> *Mother*: You'd better have that homework done by the time father comes home, otherwise I won't be responsible for what happens.
> *Child's interpretation*: Father is to be feared. Mother cannot protect me. Mother is also afraid of father. Father does not love either of us.

How might this influence the child when he grows to adulthood? It depends on a number of complex factors and the child could grow up to be a bullying and possibly violent parent, or one who overcompensates by spoiling his or her children or even be so badly affected that he or she refuses to get married at all.

Another example:

> *Parent*: If you don't eat up all your greens, I won't love you any more.
> *Child's interpretation*: I have to do things I don't want to do otherwise my parents will stop loving me.

This could have many different repercussions in the future, for example, non-assertive adults who will not express their own point of view or stand up for themselves in case people withdraw their affection. They may also grow up to be extremely dependent on what others think of them. They may also be particularly susceptible to a type of faulty thinking pattern – 'I should, I ought, I must' etc.

Who we are today – how we think, react, behave and interact with others – is dependent on our early programming. A clearer understanding of our own programmed reactions will pave the way towards forming better and more satisfying relationships with others.

'Yes, that's all fine in theory', I hear some of you mutter, 'but there's nothing wrong with my programming. The problem is with other people's programming. They are the ones that create the problems, not me.'

Any conflict involves two or more people. If you are one of them, then you may wish to reconsider the above sentiments. Each of us is responsible for our own behaviour and our own attitudes and perceptions. Unless we apply the theory to ourselves, we might as well give up now and watch television instead. Convention dictates that we tell each other not to take things personally. This is one occasion when you need to take each point personally. It is your behaviour that I am talking about and the only person who can do anything about it is you.

Summary

In order to learn new and more helpful responses, we may need to discard many of our old habits. The people we are today, our attitudes, behaviour and responses, are largely the outcome of our early programming. As these were all learnt, they can also be unlearnt. If we take the time to reflect on and use each experience as a conscious learning process, we can change our attitudes and behaviour towards conflict.

2

The anatomy of a conflict

How much more grievous are the consequences of
anger than the causes of it.

(Marcus Aurelius Antonius, 121–80 BC,
Roman emperor and philosopher)

Conflict is all about us. Sometimes it is obvious and other times it
is manifested subtly. In this chapter we will consider the nature
of conflict and the underlying philosophy of conflict resolution.
We will also examine some of the signs of conflict, both open and
hidden. Conflict also goes through different stages or levels
before reaching an obvious crisis. The timing of your intervention
is as important as your method. We will discuss the levels of
conflict and how to recognize them in order to step in before
matters come to a head.

What is conflict?

Conflict can be defined as 'a fight, a collision; a struggle, a
contest; opposition of interest, opinions or purposes; mental strife,
agony' (*Cassell Concise English Dictionary*, 1989).

Although this is a book about managing conflicts in the workplace, it seems to me that trying to divide conflicts into those that
occur at work and those that occur elsewhere is unnatural. Conflicts, whether inter or intra-personal, domestic, social or global,
are all made up of the same ingredients. The above definition

does not specify a context. Conflict management is a generic skill. Approaching people with an open and fair mind is an attitude that you display whether at home, at work or in the wider social context.

One simple definition of conflict is 'Two or more sets of needs pulling in different directions' (Cornelius et al., 1992).

Exercise

What is your definition of a conflict? You may wish to record this in your notebook.

Why does conflict arise?

People are different and so long as differences exist, conflict will arise. One of the earliest conflicts known to us is that of Cain and Abel. We cannot wipe conflict out of our lives. In fact, we would not wish to do so. Conflicting with another party is not a bad thing. Constructively managed, conflict can result in learning, growth, change, better relationships and a sense of common purpose. Indeed, playing 'devil's advocate' is doing exactly that. It ensures we have thought about the pros and cons of a situation, or the other side of the mirror, before deciding on the appropriate action. The danger lies in conflict that is badly handled or allowed to escalate.

Consider the symbol in Figure 2.1.

The symbol of the yin and the yang has its roots in ancient Chinese cosmology. The yin represents shade, the feminine side and the moon. The yang represents light, the male side of the earth and the sun. The yin force is passive, the yang aggressive. Yin and yang today is often used as a representation of balance

Figure 2.1 The symbol of the yin and the yang

between opposites. The two sides are contained within one circle to show that opposing forces often contain a part of each other. They are mutually dependent and not antagonistic.

One way to consider conflict is to see both harmony and conflict coexisting within a flowing circle. To appreciate the one, we need the other. We need both for completeness. Conflict resolution does not avoid conflict but rather welcomes it into our lives, learning from it and moving on. We do not need to avoid conflict. Rather we need to flow with it.

When we talk of conflict we often think of international conflicts. But the reason these conflicts are so intractable and corrosive is that they were not dealt with at an early enough stage. They were not embraced as an opportunity for dialogue or for closer understanding. They were allowed to intensify – passed from one generation to the next.

The multilevel theory of conflict

Any conflict will start with two opposing forces. Probably just two people. Then like a multilevel marketing scheme, it spreads downwards and outwards into an enormous pyramid shape, as in Figure 2.2.

How many people actually knew or cared about the original cause of the Montagues and Capulets' 'ancient grudge', which led to Romeo and Juliet's tragic death? Such conflicts have arisen over the centuries, resulting in heartaches, bloodshed, war and destruction. In each of the numerous wars currently raging, we can probably trace the reason back to two different points of view, two sets of values and beliefs originating centuries ago, and resulting in permanent schisms affecting nations up to this day. By now they are so huge, so entrenched, that it is almost impossible to resolve them. Each one of us in our own way could

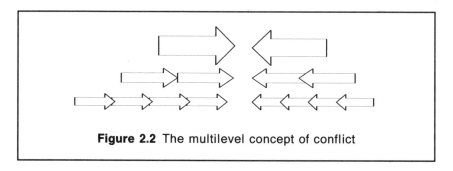

Figure 2.2 The multilevel concept of conflict

Figure 2.3 A conflict starts with two points of view

prevent such tragedies happening in the future if we could only learn how to resolve conflict early enough. Just one person can make a difference.

Now consider the picture of the pyramids if we took a helicopter view over the ages. The conflict may have started with two points of view (Figure 2.3).

Now imagine that A and B are two warring communities separated by many miles. Each community has its own traditions, dialect and culture. Their children are taught to hate each other and they, in turn, teach the next generation the same views. With the passing of years, the communities expand into villages with new houses, shops and other facilities built. Expansions normally grow in an outward circle from the centre, whereas communication continues to be directed towards the centre.

People living side by side on the peripheries originate from different centres and consider themselves to be members of an opposing community, and they maintain their original culture, dialect, traditions and hatred towards the other community.

Some people currently appear to us as to be living side by side when in fact they are living back to back (Figure 2.4). Their original differences are long forgotten but still they continue to bicker and fight amongst each other.

I recall visiting friends in a pleasant rural community for a pub lunch. I was amazed to hear my friends' derogatory remarks

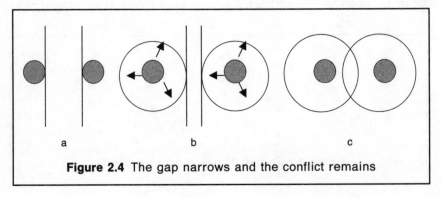

a   b   c

Figure 2.4 The gap narrows and the conflict remains

about a group of people congregating around the bar. 'They're from the next village,' they explained. 'They're all a bit weird there!' Now I noticed how often the two groups baited each other and that there was a whole host of 'racial discrimination' jokes to go with the baiting.

Curious, I asked if we could visit the infamous next village. 'Better take your passport,' they joked. 'You can borrow one of our bullet-proof vests.' We strolled to the 'next village'. I could not see where one stopped and the other started. There was no boundary. One row of houses backing onto a row of houses situated in the other village. The absurdity of the situation was lost on them.

We may consider conflicts in the workplace only in terms of victimization or harassment. Company bosses make statements like, 'We don't have a problem with conflict in our office'. They would probably not count the perpetual arguments over the office parking as worthy of note and, yet, it is exactly that sort of conflict that can intensify, causing major problems.

Conflicts often arise when we feel threatened by someone whom we perceive:

- operates from a different set of values and beliefs
- invades what we see as our territory
- takes away something we consider to be rightfully ours
- harms us or undermines us in some way
- is different from us in some way
- causes us discomfort.

Exercise

Can you think of any other reasons? Record them in your workbook.

Our primal instincts drive us to fight with, or run away from, what is unfamiliar, undesirable or threatening. This concept is fundamental to the understanding of conflict. If our natural inclination is towards fight, then we are more likely to view conflict as a contest or a competition. If our inclination is towards flight, then we will think that all conflict is bad and to be avoided at all costs. Neither of these two reactions is helpful in a conflict and we will examine how we can overcome them in a later chapter.

The hidden signs of conflict

Neil's testimony

When I took on this job last year I was invited to a meeting by Ron, the marketing manager, to whom I reported. It became apparent to me almost immediately that he and Sal, one of the product managers, did not see eye to eye. Their body language was hostile and totally at odds with what they were saying. They made very little eye contact and some of their remarks appeared quite pointed, even though they were outwardly affable. I noticed Sal doodling impatiently whenever Ron made a point. As I was sitting by her, I couldn't help sneaking a look. Her biro strokes were so hard they nearly tore the page. These feelings were later confirmed by some of my colleagues who told me it was an open secret that they could not stand each other.

Conflict is not always manifested in public disagreements, shouting or other obvious signs. Your intuition will tell you when something is not quite right. Have you ever seen someone come into a room where there had been a previous incident and use his or her fingers like scissors to indicate that the atmosphere was so thick, it could literally be cut?

Conflict can be expressed in a passive or aggressive manner, and either subtly or obviously, or any combination of the four. The model in Figure 2.5 is one way of looking at the signs or symptoms of conflict.

In Figure 2.5:

- quadrant I is an obvious sign of conflict displayed in an aggressive manner, i.e. shouting, rowing, name-calling, violence, etc.
- quadrant II is a hidden sign of conflict displayed in an aggressive manner, such as snide comments, put you downs, humiliation, constant carping and criticism etc. Hate and smear campaigns also come under this heading.
- quadrant III is a hidden sign of conflict displayed in a passive manner, such as non-cooperation, absenteeism and sickness. In one British Airways strike, a high proportion of staff went off sick, rather than openly confront management by striking.
- quadrant IV is an obvious sign of conflict displayed in a

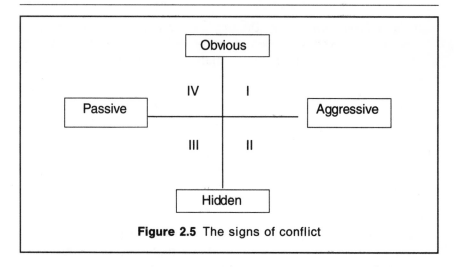

Figure 2.5 The signs of conflict

passive manner, such as exaggerated politeness, ignoring or sending to Coventry, memos pointing out the other party's errors or shortcomings with copies to bosses etc.

Exercise

Could you recognize hidden clues to conflict? Record a few examples in your workbook.

The levels of conflict

Just as there are open and hidden clues to conflict, there are also *levels* or stages of conflict to consider. Not all conflicts end in crisis, but in the event of one happening, you can be sure that the clues were there to be seen from the start.

Think of an interpersonal conflict, whether at work or else-where, that you wish you could have handled better. What was the outcome of the conflict? Did it end in a fight or a parting of the ways? Was there some sort of *crisis* that you associate with it? A crisis in a conflict could be a divorce, being dismissed, attend-ing an industrial tribunal or grievance process, resigning your job, a fight involving verbal or physical violence, or even a war. You can often identify this stage in a conflict by completing the sentence 'matters reached crisis point when...'.

Think back to the very beginning of the conflict. This may take some reflection but try to identify the first moment you became aware that something was not quite right. You see? Most conflicts start with nothing more than a feeling of *discomfort*. A feeling that something is not quite right.

Try to track the conflict stages from the initial feelings of *discomfort* to the *crisis*. You may find that an incident took place sometime after you first became aware of the discomfort. It could have been a very small *incident* and you probably ignored it, thinking it was not worth worrying about. Or you may have experienced concern but decided not to pursue it for fear of looking as if you were making a mountain out of a molehill.

But the incident left a bad taste in your mouth. It left a *misunderstanding* that was never clarified and brought out into the open. It left you somewhat cautious and wary of the other person.

And then you became uneasy about that person. Subtly your manner changed and the other person picked it up. Still, nothing was said but the *tension* was palpable. It affected not only the two of you but others around you as well.

We all know what happens when emotions are not dealt with appropriately. One day they explode. And so the inevitable happened and you finally came to the *crisis*.

The journey from discomfort to crisis can take a day, a week, a month, a year or several years (see Figure 2.6). What is certain is

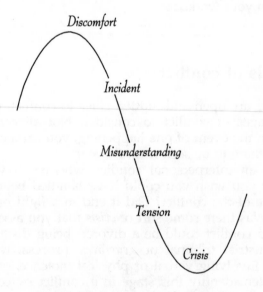

Figure 2.6 The levels of conflict

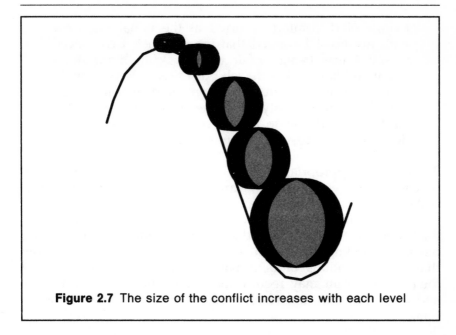

Figure 2.7 The size of the conflict increases with each level

that if you do not deal with these feelings at the time they will fester and eventually erupt. Like a boil, a great deal of unpleasant matter will be released and, sadly, if left to this stage is likely to leave a scar.

The journey from discomfort to crisis may be likened to a snowball hurtling down a snow-clad slope. As it gathers momentum and rolls down, so it becomes larger and more out of control (see Figure 2.7).

Be aware of a possible impending conflict as soon as your antennae pick up the first faint signal of discomfort. Attend to those feelings and establish why they have surfaced. You may choose not to do anything at the time but at least you are alert and monitoring the situation. With each stage of development, emotions become stronger and intervention more difficult. The situation can quickly spiral out of control.

Heather's story

Four years ago I took a well-paid job as a senior PA with a prestigious firm of chartered surveyors. I left 18 months later when I couldn't stand my boss's continued possessiveness and sexual harassment any longer. It was only when reflecting on the above levels of conflict that I admitted to myself that my first twinge of discomfort occurred at the initial interview with my boss! I wanted that job so much I convinced myself I was being unfair to him. With hindsight, I might still have taken the job but I would have thought it through more carefully and prepared myself to deal with him more firmly from the outset. I learned the hard way and had to take a year off between jobs to deal with the stress and trauma it caused me.

There is an appropriate set of skills to deal with each level of conflict, so you need to learn to identify them accurately. Notice that two people who are involved in a conflict may be experiencing different levels of conflict. While you are at the discomfort stage, the other party might be experiencing misunderstanding or tension. It is often only at the crisis stage that the perceptions of both parties coincide! If you wait till then, the problem may require the intervention of a third party and even that may not resolve the issue to everyone's satisfaction.

Timing your intervention

When you choose to intervene is as important as *how* you choose to respond. It is better to respond appropriately at an early stage. The longer a situation is left to fester, the more complicated it becomes and the stronger our emotions. Thus, when we finally have no option but to confront it, we may say things and act in a manner we later regret.

So, for example:

1. At the level of discomfort, we should be on the alert and use our analysis skills to understand the situation.
2. An incident would bring into play our empathy and communication skills. Talking over the incident and perhaps agreeing that it need not happen again.
3. At the point of misunderstanding, we need to look at our own part in the problem. How much of our own beliefs, attitude and personal issues may be contributing?
4. During the tension period, we need to examine our own emotions and find ways of calming them in a healthy fashion.
5. If we allow matters to develop into crisis, we may find the situation is beyond our skills and a neutral mediator could be brought in to assist.

You may not always choose to confront an issue face on at a very early stage. But if you are at least aware of the possibility that you are on the slippery slope to a confrontation then you have the time to formulate a strategy to avert a crisis. You can become more aware of your own part in the situation and change your tactics or response. Otherwise, you might inadvertently be provoking or prolonging a conflict.

There is no right or wrong tool to use and no single prescribed way to intervene – it depends on the very nature of the conflict. For example, empathy-building and a win/win attitude may help avert a misunderstanding. If a misunderstanding does occur, mapping the problem may be appropriate. By the time you have finished reading this book, you will have a valuable set of tools to help you deal confidently with any conflict situation.

We need be flexible and adaptable in our repertoire. If something does not work, we can always use another. Trying and failing is nobler than not trying at all.

Finding the opportunity in conflict

Conflict can be a catalyst for change. We can regard it as an opportunity to learn about another point of view, to understand a different perspective. If we all agreed with each other, there would be no impetus for change. As George Bernard Shaw pointed out in *Man and Superman*, 'All change depends on unreasonable people, because they try to adapt the world to themselves, whereas reasonable people try to adapt themselves to the world around them'.

Therefore, we can choose to look for the opportunity in conflict and turn it to our advantage or we can regard it as a danger, something to be avoided at all costs. Next time you are in a meeting and a potential conflict arises, try thinking: 'Oh good, someone is expressing a different point of view. What an opportunity to explore the issue in greater detail.' Your attitude and your genuine interest in the other point of view will create debate and will encourage others to deal with it positively as well.

Summary

We can view conflict as being part of one flowing whole, the dark side and the bright side of nature. If conflict is not resolved, it can grow downwards and outwards in a pyramid shape, infecting future generations with its poison. We need to try to stop conflict before it becomes a crisis. We also need to be aware of the hidden signs of conflict so that we become attuned to picking up subtle signals and able to act on them. Conflict offers the possibility of growth. If resolved satisfactorily and at an early enough stage, the opportunity can be taken to learn from it.

3

Conflict in the workplace

> Why is there no conflict at this meeting? Something's wrong when there is no conflict.
>
> (Michael Eisner, Disney Corporation chief)

In this chapter we will begin to apply our conflict-resolving mindset to conflict at work and examine the signs that point to conflict or impending conflict in the workplace.

There are many possible sources of conflict in the workplace, and a combination of many different elements and protagonists. However, conflict resolution skills are generic. Very often people become embroiled in the details of the conflict – the 'what is it about?' What is more important is to develop your analysis skills to recognize the needs and concerns of the parties involved. In this way, you will be able to choose the appropriate tool for the conflict with which you are dealing.

There are two possible ways in which you might be involved in conflict at work: directly and indirectly.

1. *Direct involvement*: a conflict has arisen between you and another party or parties. Here your own mindset and skills will be fully stretched. Many people find it more difficult to resolve a conflict in which they are directly involved than one in which they act as third party.
2. *Indirect involvement*: a conflict between your bosses, colleagues, subordinates, various departments, or between customers and

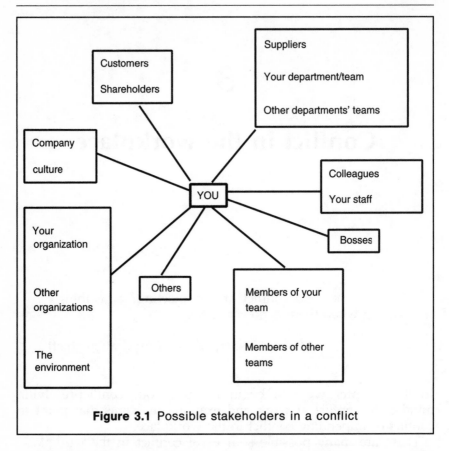

Figure 3.1 Possible stakeholders in a conflict

your organization. Although not involved directly, you might find yourself called upon to mediate.

To obtain a fuller picture of the complexity of conflict in the workplace, it is useful to build a diagram of the 'stakeholders' (Figure 3.1).

Any of the parties in Figure 3.1 could also be involved in conflict with each other and this may directly or indirectly affect you or your team.

The universe as a system

Underlying the philosophy of conflict resolution presented in this book is systemic thinking. This also forms an important part of the beliefs and values of NLP and is related to the study of cybernetics (the science of control and communication systems within machines and animals).

The connection between cybernetics and human behaviour is often attributed to Dr Maxwell Maltz (1960). If we believe that the universe with all its complex components is a system, just as our body/mind/spirit is one system, then we may appreciate how any change in one small component effectively changes the whole system.

Let us consider change within organizations. We all react differently to change – some of us embrace it, some tolerate it and some actively resist it. But those of us who are able to adapt and display creative responses will have the advantage. The rest of us will be swept out with the old systems.

Put simply, the person with the most flexibility in their behaviour has the widest range of choices in influencing the system. It also means that each and every one of us *can* make a difference. By changing my attitude, I also change other people's attitudes.

> *Change begins with*
> *ME*

There is an old story of four blind men and an elephant. None of them knew what an elephant was and they were asked to feel one and describe it. The first blind man felt the elephant's tail. It was long, coarse and with tufts at the end, so he concluded that an elephant was a rope. The second man felt one of the elephant's legs. It was solid and round and rather rough, so he thought an elephant must be a tree. The third man felt the elephant's side. It was huge, flat and textured. He concluded an elephant was a wall. The last man felt the elephant's trunk. This was long, flexible and smooth, so he concluded that an elephant was a snake. None of the four men was able to see the whole elephant.

Conflict resolution involves seeing the *whole elephant*. We cannot know individual parts of a complete system and assume we understand it all. A system is more than the sum of its parts. Any change in the balance or relationships between any of the components will inevitably produce changes in other parts. This is where organizations so often go wrong. Changes are made in one part of a system without adequate exploration and communication of the repercussions in other parts.

As a manager, you need to understand this principle. A boardroom brawl can never be kept secret for long because of the repercussions it will have on every other part of the system. A conflict within one team can have grave implications for other teams and for the productivity and effectiveness of the organization as a whole.

Alison's testimony

As part of my responsibilities, I had to present a weekly report to my manager. The information I submitted formed part of my boss's management report to the board. My report depended on figures from the accounts and sales departments. I noticed that the information from sales was arriving later and later and kept pressing Jane (who was responsible) to let me have the printouts on time. Finally, after one of our reports missed the board meeting deadline, my boss, Mandy, called me in and severely admonished me. She was simply not interested in the fact that I couldn't produce the report without the sales figures. The delayed report had caused our divisional director to receive a formal reprimand from the board and he, in turn, had reprimanded her. Mandy said it was my problem and I had to rectify it.

I decided to ask Jane out for a drink one lunch time to discover the reason for the delays. After a couple of glasses of wine she confessed that Alan, the sales director, had instructed her to delay the printouts on purpose. She said he resented Mandy because she had caused him to appear insignificant at a meeting a few weeks previously. I could hardly believe what I was hearing. It brought home to me how much we all depended on each other to complete our work.

Allied to this philosophy is that we need to balance our working lives with our personal lives. We cannot walk into our offices and somehow transform ourselves into different people with no personal lives. We may be professional and we may strive to ensure that 'the show goes on', however, conflict, stress or imbalance at home will have an effect on your work and vice versa. A change made in one environment will also cause change in another. Gandhi once observed that we cannot 'do right in one department of life whilst attempting to do wrong in another department. Life is one indivisible whole' (quoted in Fischer, 1962).

Company culture and our values and beliefs

We all have our own values and beliefs even if we are not consciously aware of their effects on our daily lives. Every outcome we achieve, every decision we make, and our attitudes and behaviour, all depend on our values and beliefs. If we consider the source of much conflict and stress at work, we will observe how often a clash of values or cultures is responsible.

Organizations, too, have their own specific cultures. This is loosely defined as 'the way we do things around here'. When we move from one company to another, we first need to accustom ourselves to the different culture.

Even if an organization provides new staff with induction training, it is highly unlikely that the training will consciously include mention of the culture. Sometimes when talking about systems and procedures, they may mention their own preferred way of doing things. This is what culture is.

How can you identify your own organizational culture (OC)? There are a number of different tools that can help you decide how you perceive the culture.

Exercise

1. Draw a picture that represents your organization.
2. If your organization were an animal, what would it be?
3. What are some of the tales or folklore of your organization?
4. How would you describe your organization if you were talking to an outsider?
5. Would you recognize your company from the wording of a job recruitment advertisement?
6. Where is senior management located? Do they have their own facilities? How do people dress? How do they interact?
7. How often do you see the senior managers? Do they recognize everyone?
8. Do you believe you and your organization are well matched? Give your reasons.
9. Identify two people in your organization who are a good match with your OC and two people who are not. Briefly note down the reasons for your choice.

The answers to these will help you build up a picture of your organization's culture. Give it a creative name or simply think of other similar organizations. What traits do they share?

Organizational culture and conflict

Organizations have their own rules and regulations, values and beliefs. In what way might these cause conflicts in the organization? Three common causes have been identified: not walking the talk, mismatch between individual and company values and beliefs, and the psychological contract.

Not walking the talk

Often an organization will declare its supposed values and beliefs, say in a mission statement or customer documentation, while acting in a contrary manner. Espoused values and those by which organizations actually operate may differ widely.

For example, a company may declare to its customers and shareholders that 'the customer comes first'. And yet its customer services department may be understaffed, and undervalued, instructed to refute customer complaints or to haggle with them when they ask for perfectly legitimate refunds or compensation. This can be a source of internal conflict for the employees.

Another example could be where a company declares that it is an equal opportunities employer. Statements are pinned to the wall, they appear on recruitment advertising, press releases and media declarations, but employees can see the truth for themselves. Promotions may be gender or racially biased and opportunities for the disabled limited. The espoused values may have been the very carrots that attracted staff to the company but once they are there, they are sadly disappointed.

Mismatch between individual and company values and beliefs

We can imagine the mismatch between a bureaucratic suit-and-tie-clad employee who joins a jeans and sweatshirt media consultancy, or the incongruence of creative, non-conformists used to working their own hours to complete projects (even if it means working through the night) taken on by the Civil Service. Even small mismatches can cause serious conflict.

Even more profound are mismatches between a company's values and beliefs, and those of an individual. For example, you may have very strong feelings about experimentation on animals, or about child labour or environmental issues. If your company is involved in any of these, you have a real dilemma. Jobs are scarce these days and if you have to compromise your values, you are likely to resent the organization, again resulting in conflict.

A great deal of conflict has also been created with the move to privatization and the introduction of entrepreneurial culture into organizations such as the National Health Service or Social Services. This has resulted in loss of morale, which has reduced productivity.

The psychological contract

Most employees will expect to be given a written contract at the start of their employment, but there is another unwritten contract that exists as well – the implied psychological contract. It covers a range of expectations of rights and privileges, duties and obligations between the employer and the employee.

An employee may, for example, expect that the employer will treat staff with respect and demonstrate an understanding attitude towards personal problems, but this would not normally be stated in a contract of employment. The organization will also have a set of expectations, perhaps that the employee will be honest, show loyalty to the organization and work diligently.

Such expectations will rarely be fully met; however, a significant mismatch between the two is likely to cause misunderstandings, conflict and stress. Assumptions are made by both parties. It is useful to remember that 'to assume' makes an:

> Ass out of U and ME.

Exercise

Identify possible impending conflicts in your organization resulting from the three common factors. Can you think of any way to avert a clash arising from these?

The symptoms of organizational conflict

Imagine an organization where everyone was so keen not to disagree, to fall in with every suggestion, that changes were never discussed. What type of an organization would that be?

The organization should encourage an atmosphere of trust and open communication where opinions can be expressed honestly and issues are open to debate. For this to happen, the managerial top tier has to take the lead. Many organizational conflicts start at boardroom level. This soon filters down and out, with employees and departments taking sides and increasing the conflicts by 'stoking the fires from down below'.

What signs might point to conflict in your organization? Here are some common indicators:

- The right hand does not know what the left hand is doing.
- Communications increasingly taking the form of memos and e-mails.
- More people working behind closed doors.
- Meetings that do not achieve anything.
- 'Them and us' language.
- Interpersonal friction/hostility.
- Raised voices and tears.
- Huddles.
- Long lunch hours and poor timekeeping.
- Sickness/absenteeism.
- Low morale/tension.
- People looking glum and stressed.
- Work output/quality affected.

Exercise

Now add some of your own.

Some of the above, some of the time, are almost part and parcel of organizational life. If any of the above seem to be on the increase or are lasting longer than usual, then it is time for someone to intervene and confront the issue.

Exercise

List any symptoms of organizational stress that you identify within your organization.

Where are conflicts at work likely to occur? When reading about traffic incidents in the newspaper, we often hear the phrase 'It was an accident just waiting to happen'. In other words, the people around identified a set of circumstances that was sooner or later likely to result in an accident. With hindsight, we can often say that we expected a conflict to arise between the protagonists and yet we did nothing to prevent or avert the crisis.

Some of the more common causes of traffic incidents are:

- lack of due care and attention
- driving too fast
- driving too slowly/dithering
- not giving way
- determination to overtake
- determination not to let another car overtake you
- showing off
- driving at someone's tail
- not observing the Highway Code
- inconsiderate/aggressive driving
- losing control
- ignoring common courtesy to other drivers.

If we substitute ourselves for the cars, we can see the similarity in behaviour that leads to conflict.

Where are conflicts between people most likely to occur in an organization? Since conflict is about interaction, we need to look at where people interact and where interactions bring up differences. For example:

1. *Internal boundaries*: where roles, tasks, limits of authority or responsibilities overlap, or where they clash, are not clearly defined or are duplicated. This often happens when we forget to consider 'the whole elephant'. If we think about our own roles in isolation, without connecting them to the bigger picture, we may find ourselves in this situation. This can also be a result of the 'If it ain't broke, don't fix it' mentality where no regular management reviews of systems and procedures are carried out.
2. *External boundaries*: where direct contact is made between staff and clients, suppliers, contractors or consultants. In hierarchical companies, indirect communication may be substituted for direct contact. Staff may be instructed to talk to internal and external customers via a third party. This can often cause delays, misunderstanding and frustration.

3. *Territorial boundaries*: desks, office space, shared work space or office facilities all come under this heading. Another source of conflict is the office car park where even the most placid of people are transformed into lions defending their dens.

4. *Material goods/resources*: shared resources (photocopier, fax machine) or inequality in distribution of status resources such as mobile phones or laptop computers. A new cause of conflict is the trend towards 'hot desking' where people are no longer allocated their own desks but share office space wherever it is available. Although the idea is fashionable and may save some money, the psychological impact and the squabbles over space are likely to cause many more problems than were at first realized.

5. *Weak/poor management*: lack of strategy, no shared vision, poor communication and an unsound organizational structure all cause conflict. This can lead to power struggles as people perceive an opportunity to advance themselves at the expense of others.

6. *Lack of professional management training*: many managers may have been promoted on length of service or technical competence and are simply not equipped to deal with people and with today's workplace problems.

7. *Leadership/management styles*: the way in which the company is led and the individual management styles can cause enormous conflicts. An abrasive chief executive, for example, may annoy many people even if initially perceived as the best change that ever happened to the company. A non-assertive manager can cause just as many problems as one using 'Rottweiler' techniques.

8. *Poor decision-making processes*: how decisions are made and by whom can reveal a great deal about a company. Are decisions made democratically or autocratically? Are staff consulted on matters that affect them or are they simply told? Do they have to wait for ages for a decision or can they rely on a speedy reply? Effective decision-making is a skill and an integral part of management development.

9. *Poor interpersonal skills*: some companies neglect this aspect of training in their staff development programmes. The education system in the United Kingdom does little to encourage thinking or articulation skills. Scant attention is paid to improving interaction and interpersonal skills. One of the constant laments of recruiters is that even graduates lack the most basic social skills.

10. *Poor change management*: effective change management could minimize any conflict arising. Introducing change to any aspect of an organization requires careful planning, communication and management. Change needs to be planned with military precision yet more people bungle it than any other management process.
11. *Inequality among staff*: conditions of work, salary, hours, benefits and so on can cause massive resentment and conflicts in a workplace. Racism, sexism, ageism and whatever new 'ism' is in vogue are others.

It is not possible to list every source of conflict in an office. Every day and with every trend, new issues emerge. We cannot expect, nor do we want to encourage, a conflict-free office. Nevertheless conflicts are going to occur and it is up to us whether we handle them effectively, learn from them and move on or whether the conflict increases and causes great damage to the company's productivity, effectiveness, profit and reputation.

Exercise

Consider the following questions:

1. Do I have any unresolved issues with anyone from the past?
2. With whom am I likely to have problems in the future?
3. What are the likely issues?
4. What steps can I take now to avert or resolve these issues?

Summary

In this chapter we took a closer look at some of the elements connected with conflict at work. We considered our own involvement, direct or indirect, and the possible stakeholders in the conflict. We viewed the concept of the universe as a system and how little sense it made to isolate certain aspects of a conflict without taking the 'whole elephant' into consideration.

We also examined company culture and values and the hidden signs that reveal conflict in organizations. Finally, we listed possible sources of conflict at work to enable you to identify your own and take corrective action.

Part II

The skills of conflict resolution

4

Developing a win/win approach

... everybody, every team, every platform, every division, every component is there not for individual competitive profit or recognition, but for contribution to the system as a whole on a win/win basis.

(W. Edwards Deming, 1900–93, US quality guru)

In this chapter we will consider our attitudes and behaviour in conflict situations. Why do we react the way we do? Is there a better way? This leads on to an explanation of the principles of a win/win approach and a more satisfactory method of dealing with conflict.

How do we behave in conflict? Let us start by examining how people behave in conflict and why. Understanding how we and others behave will help us to choose a more appropriate response.

Here are some unhelpful behaviours which are often exhibited in conflict:

- shouting
- insulting/cursing
- humiliating
- making accusations
- bringing up the past
- sulking
- tears
- withdrawing
- physical violence

- avoidance
- pretending it is not happening
- 'giving the cold shoulder'
- becoming resentful
- bottling up our emotions
- storming off in a huff
- taking revenge/back-stabbing.

Exercise

Do you have any examples? Add your own.

Some behaviours are useful in resolving conflict and others are not. Most of us know this but, when confronted with a conflict, we often display inappropriate behaviour. Why should this be?

To understand just why this happens, we need to look at our fight/flight stress response mechanism. The following is a simplified explanation of our bodies' very complex and extremely sophisticated survival mechanism.

Our bodies are designed to react to unusual or excessive demands, threats or challenges to ensure our survival. The alarm reaction resides in one of the oldest part of our brains and is a primitive response designed to prepare caveman and woman to cope with life-threatening events, such as confronting a wild animal.

In such a confrontation, a split-second decision would be required and there would be no time to think things through logically. It is almost as though another being takes command of our bodies on our behalf, orchestrating a defence campaign. Our brain, sensing the danger, assesses the situation swiftly and sends instructions to the body to prepare it to run away or stay and fight the enemy. The brain works out the most appropriate response and sends impulses to various parts of the body to prepare it for action.

What does happen to our bodies?

- Our adrenal glands produce certain hormones in specific quantities to aid us either to flee or to stay and fight.
- The liver produces more fuel for energy.
- We breathe faster and deeper to take in more oxygen.
- Our pupils dilate to enable us to see better in the dark.
- Our senses are sharpened and our alertness is increased.

- Our digestive system slows down or closes completely.
- Our mouths go dry.
- Our hearts beat much faster to pump blood round the body.
- We sweat to reduce skin temperature.
- Blood diverts from the surface of the skin to minimize bleeding, if injured.
- Our muscles strengthen and tense and fists clench ready to spring into action.

These actions indicate what happens to our bodies when faced with a threat. What we need to bear in mind is that conflict, or the threat of it, will give rise to the very same symptoms. When faced with a conflict, our bodies prepare to act. This instinctive reaction depends on the specific message from the brain to the nervous system. But since this depends on our perception of an event, we can re-educate our systems to enable us to behave in a more appropriate manner.

The alarm response helps our bodies jolt into action. Once the appropriate action has been taken, then another system steps in, bringing us back to our normal state, or homeostasis as it is known.

Imagine that your boss storms into your office with a furious look on his face. Your brain will first register what is happening to alert you. Then a quick scan of your memory occurs, like a super-computer running through its files, in literally nanoseconds: have we any previous experience of this, or anything similar, happening? Depending on the answer, signals will be sent quickly via nerve impulses to every part of your body to prepare you for the coming action. If the conclusion is reassuring, (He has come in to moan that someone has taken his parking space ... again!), then the general alert does not continue to the alarm stage.

If, for any reason, your brain cannot match this to a previous experience, or decides that you might be in trouble, then it sends your body into a state of alarm. Specific hormones will take over to help you deal with the situation and, depending on the cocktail of hormones released, you may deal with it aggressively on a like-for-like basis or you may just wish you could run away and hide till it was all over.

This is the point, though, where you *can* quickly assess and evaluate your feelings. '*Is this an appropriate response?*' From there you can begin to deal with the conflict calmly and reasonably.

Returning to our behaviour in conflict, which of the previous examples are 'fight' behaviour and which are 'flight'? (See Table 4.1.)

Table 4.1 Examples of 'fight' and 'flight' behaviours

Examples of fight behaviour	Examples of flight behaviour
Shouting	Withdrawal
Violence	Denial
Slamming doors	Giving in
Name-calling	Crying
Now add your own:	Now add your own:

You may find that some behaviour could represent either fight *or* flight. For example, crying could be a passive behaviour or could be used to manipulate, which is an example of aggressive behaviour. The difference is in the *intention* behind the behaviour.

Exercise

Consider your own behaviour in conflict. List in your workbook the five different behaviours you use most of all. Do not write down what you know you *should* do. Write down what you actually do.

Now compare your reactions to the list above and tick whether they fall into the fight or flight pattern of behaviours. You probably already have a good inkling of your tendencies. This exercise will make you more aware of how you are displaying them.

What is the intention or message behind 'fight' behaviour? We might be looking to blame someone or to punish. We could be threatening. It could be symptomatic of an 'I'm right, you're wrong' mindset. Perhaps the clearest message of all is *'I win, you lose'*.

What is the intention or message behind 'flight' behaviour? This could be to keep the peace or to avoid conflict altogether. It could be a lack of self-esteem or an 'I'm wrong, you're right' mindset. The clear signal here is *'I lose, you win'*.

Both behaviours are examples of reactions, not responses. When we react, we listen to ourselves. When we respond we listen to others. Reactions produce winners and losers, and if the 1970s pop group ABBA is to be believed, then the winner takes it all. Hardly conducive to resolving conflict! Is there another way?

In reacting to conflict, we fall into fight or flight behaviour. In responding to conflict we can transform this into a third alternative: flow.

- Fight behaviour – aggressive – win/lose.
- Flight behaviour – passive – lose/win (or lose/lose).
- Flow behaviour – assertive – win/win.

This behaviour is called *flow* to indicate its fluidity and flexibility. It is elegant, graceful and surefooted – like a ballet dancer. It demonstrates a reasoned, compassionate and empathetic response. Here, we do not try and score points off each other or win at the expense of the other person. The approach is 'how can we both win here?' 'How can we ensure that both our needs are largely met?' Flow behaviour, or assertiveness, is a skill which can be developed in us all.

Let us take an example of a colleague who publicly accused you of stirring up trouble and undermining others. You could choose to:

- fight – explode, shout back, become abusive or use violence, seek your revenge, start a hate campaign.
- flight – burst into tears, suppress your distress, withdraw, avoid the issue, appeal to others, apologize unnecessarily.
- flow – contain your discomfort, seek to explore, withdraw to consider needs and concerns, stay calm while seeking further explanation.

And yet people often continue to display unhelpful behaviour when faced with conflict even when they know that there may be a better way. You may hear someone saying 'I simply can't help it' or 'I just saw red'. This is faulty thinking and a disempowering pattern. We all have control over our responses and we have a choice.

As previously demonstrated, our learned response is a pattern which we have developed over the years due to a faulty learning cycle. We can condition ourselves into a particular response so that it becomes an unconscious habit, either positive or negative. Once we adopt this pattern, it is difficult to unlearn and so we continue the cycle, often with disastrous results.

Is all fight/flight behaviour harmful? The answer is a resounding 'No'. For example, if threatened by someone with a gun, this would not be the time to use our assertiveness skills and it would serve our purposes in the short term to use fight or flight behaviour. What is important is that we do so consciously and realize that we have a choice. There may be long-term and short-term benefits and we should take these into account.

There are two important elements in a conflict: the issue and the people involved. Let us examine how our specific behaviours affect these two elements.

Exercise

Consider two or three examples of behaviour in each of the three categories, fight, flight and flow (Table 4.2). Now follow this format in your workbook to consider the effects of each set of behaviours on the issue and on the people involved.

You may notice a pattern emerging (Figure 4.1) on the way in which each set of behaviours deals with the issue and with the people involved.

Table 4.2 Examples of 'fight', 'flight' and 'flow' behaviours

Specific examples of behaviour	Strengths (long and short term)	Weaknesses (long and short term)	How it affects the people involved	How it affects the issue involved
Fight:				
Flight:				
Flow:				

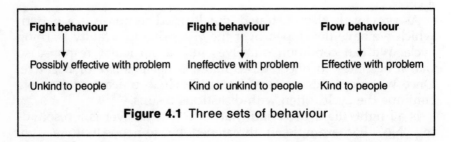

Fight behaviour	Flight behaviour	Flow behaviour
↓	↓	↓
Possibly effective with problem	Ineffective with problem	Effective with problem
Unkind to people	Kind or unkind to people	Kind to people

Figure 4.1 Three sets of behaviour

In fight behaviour, the intention is to resolve the issue with little regard for the feelings or welfare of the people concerned. It is always unkind to the people involved and is ineffective in the long term, even if it appears effective in the short term.

In flight behaviour, the issue is often not properly thought through. This can cause considerable annoyance to the people concerned. It is ineffective on the issue and can be either kind or unkind to the people involved, depending on the specific reaction.

Turning to flow behaviour, we note that the intention is to resolve the issue while being gentle with the people concerned.

In conflict resolution language, you may hear the phrases 'soft' and 'hard' used in place of 'ineffective' and 'kind'. This would offer the following template:

- Win/lose: hard/soft on the issue, hard on the people.
- Lose/win: soft on the issue, hard/soft on the people.
- Win/win: hard on the issue, soft on the people.

I call this the spider in the bath response. If you go into your bathroom and find a large spider sitting at the bottom of the bath you have at least three choices available to you:

1. Find a newspaper. Roll it up. Bring it down with all your force and flatten the unfortunate creature.
2. Recoil in horror and run away. Refuse to return to the bathroom until someone removes the spider or it decides on a change of scenery.
3. Unfold the newspaper and gently coax the spider onto it. Carry the newspaper, complete with spider, to the nearest door or window and let it go.

The first option is the aggressive one. You have dealt with the issue but you were somewhat unkind to the poor spider. The second option is passive. You have dealt with neither the issue nor with the spider. The third option is assertive. You have dealt with the issue and have also been gentle with the spider.

The issue was not the spider, but its presence in the bath. Dealing with the issue and separating it from the people concerned is a cornerstone of the win/win approach. One way to do this is to ensure that you are objective and unemotional when approaching a problem and not labelling the person involved. For example, 'Your last report contained a number of inaccuracies.' compared with 'You are sloppy'.

In dealing with conflict, confusing the issue by bringing up irrelevant past incidents is a common failing. A useful way to keep the dialogue to the matter in hand is to say, *'let's return to the issue in question'* or *'How does this relate to the issue in question?'*

The principles of win/win

There is a well-known tale of two sisters and one orange. Both sisters wanted the orange and were squabbling over who would receive it. What could they do?

If you said 'cut it in half', you'll be pleased to know that is exactly what they did. However, one sister used her half for juice and found there was not enough to quench her thirst. The other sister grated the rind for a cake recipe and found she had insufficient to bake her cake. Each sister had half an orange, when, in effect, they could each have had the whole orange.

What could the sisters have done to get what they both wanted? The answer lies in one word: *needs*. They could have explored their needs and communicated them to each other before settling on a solution.

For a win/win approach to happen, the golden rule is:

> *Needs first*
> *Solutions later*

In the orange story, the two sisters reached a *compromise*. This is often mistaken for a win/win result. In fact, a compromise is more often lose/lose or win/lose.

Let us identify the advantages of a compromise:

- It may be considered fair.
- It is often the simplest solution.
- If we cannot increase the size of the pie, we can share what is available.
- Each party will have at least some of its needs met.
- It makes for an easier life.
- It takes less time.

And the disadvantages?

- One party usually has to give more.
- The person who gives more may still feel aggrieved.

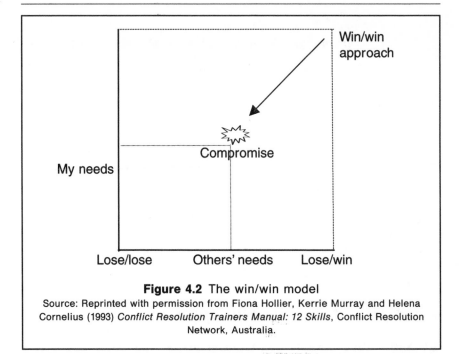

Figure 4.2 The win/win model

Source: Reprinted with permission from Fiona Hollier, Kerrie Murray and Helena Cornelius (1993) *Conflict Resolution Trainers Manual: 12 Skills*, Conflict Resolution Network, Australia.

- There may be less commitment to the solution.
- It does not give an opportunity to examine fully all available options.
- It may harm the relationship through resentment or bitterness.
- It may still be a lose/lose situation

Figure 4.2 illustrates the difference between win/win and compromise. The vertical axis represents how much of our own needs are being met. The horizontal axis represents how much of others' needs are being met.

If we aim to have all our needs met and none of the others', then we are adopting an aggressive win/lose approach. ('Only one of us is going to win here, and that's me!')

If we aim to have all others' needs met and none of our own, we are adopting a passive lose/win approach. ('Never mind, I'm not important. Have it your way and pardon me for breathing!')

If we opt for what many people would consider fair, and aim for a halfway point between the two, that is compromise. Compromise does not necessarily imply that half of each of our needs is met. Indeed, a compromise could be 1 per cent of one person's needs and 99 per cent of the others'. Here is the second golden rule of the win/win approach:

> *Compromise should always be the last resort.*

Compromise does no more than take into account some of each of the parties' needs.

In Figure 4.2, notice that if we move from the lose/lose point to compromise, we have neglected a huge expanse of possible solutions. If, instead, we start by exploring 100 per cent of both needs, then we are adopting a win/win approach. Notice that a win/win *approach* is not necessarily a win/win *solution*. We may, in fact, return to compromise when all the issues have been explored in depth. But when we work backwards from the win/win approach point, we are likely to have many more satisfying solutions. Moreover, each party will feel that honour has been satisfied and will be more likely to implement the agreed solution.

Principles of the win/win approach

In competitive sports, there are winners and there are losers. Only the winner receives the gold medal. In real life, though, this does not always have to be the case.

Exercise

Try this as a training activity. Ask a group to divide into pairs and sit opposite each other with a table between them. Put a £1 coin on the table and give the following instructions: 'Whoever slides the coin to their side earns a point. Now in 30 seconds, let's see how many points you can win.' In my experience, the game becomes one of 'snatch the coin' and much merriment ensues.

At the end of the activity, ask 'how many points did each of you earn?' and the answer often indicates a 'win/lose' attitude and a lowish score, i.e., 'I have seven but Jane only managed three'. Now ask the participants what their aim was and most will say to win as many points as possible. And in order to win, they assumed that the other person had to lose.

Had they adopted a win/win mindset, they would have realized that the quickest way to win the most points would be for each party to put a finger lightly on the coin and slide it to either side in turn. The faster they slid the coin, the more points they would earn – together. This activity generates a great deal of reflection about our own mindsets.

A win/win approach is to want what is fair for all parties involved – ensuring your own needs are met and that others' needs are met too. We need to change a possible mindset: that in order for us to win, someone else must lose.

Win/win is respecting relationships and considering others' needs, concerns, interests, perspectives and emotions. To achieve win/win you need consultation, a high level of trust and open communication. When such an approach is chosen, our energies are focused on finding high-quality solutions, not bickering and trying to 'put one over'.

Very often a conflict appears to be irreconcilable because of the very different positions taken by the conflicting parties. The two sisters' positions were fixed – each wanted the orange – but their needs were different. We often think that different interests lead to conflict when, in fact, their very difference is what often leads us to the solution.

David's story

> We are four people working together in a fairly confined space. Two members of the department were constantly arguing over the central heating. Stella generally arrived first and immediately switched off the radiator. After a while, Tom would notice the cold and switch it back on. It sounds so trivial but this went on for a couple of days and angry words were exchanged. One day, exasperated, I suggested that they wear lighter/heavier clothing in the office. 'It's not that,' said Stella. 'The air is so dry in the office with the radiator on, that it has affected my nose and throat and they are both now badly inflamed.' Purely by chance we understood the problem, and resolved the conflict by purchasing a humidifier. It sounds so obvious in retrospect but at the time we didn't think to ask and Stella didn't think to explain.

Uncovering needs

Because we are not used to thinking about needs, they can often be difficult to uncover. A useful way to adopt a 'needs' mindset is by consciously identifying your own needs in various situations and articulating them to yourself. Here are some useful tips for identifying other people's needs in a conflict situation:

1. *Explain what needs are and why they matter.* It may sound simple but we should never assume that people have ascertained their own needs. Nor should we assume that they can see its relevance to a conflict. Spell out that we are looking for a solution that will allow everyone to have as many needs met as possible.
2. *Shift from solutions to needs.* When we ask people what they need, they usually reply by giving a solution masquerading as a need, e.g. 'I need my own office', when the actual need is for privacy, quiet or status. There could be a variety of solutions to meet this need. 'My own office' is only one of the possibilities. Ask what benefit they will derive from their stated need. That often reveals the true need behind the request.
3. *Ask 'Why?'* When people present you with their solutions, ask why they need it, e.g, a request by one of your staff for a mobile phone could indicate a need for recognition of status or a genuine need to be contactable while on the road.
4. *Ascertain their concerns.* If you were in their position, would your needs, interests or solutions be acceptable? What are their reservations or fears in implementing a solution? You can do this either by asking directly or, if impractical or inappropriate, by putting yourself in their shoes and trying to see their position. You should also ask: 'What would happen if this need were not met?'
5. *Listen.* Use listening skills to draw them out, summarizing and checking as you go along. We will be discussing active listening in more detail in a later chapter.
6. *Do not confuse your own needs with those of others.* When assessing the other person's needs, do not confuse them with your own, e.g., 'That person needs to be on time' is your need and not theirs. They may not feel the need to be on time at all!
7. *Encourage them to be more specific.* If, for example, an intangible need is identified, i.e. the need for recognition or respect, ask them: 'What would it take for you to feel (recognized, respected)?'
8. *Establish as many needs as possible.* Most of us will have more than one simple need behind a position. If a need is complex, we may need to divide it into smaller parts, e.g., 'I need more

freedom to make decisions'. We could break this into smaller needs, e.g., 'freedom to make decisions in a particular field or up to a particular monetary limit'. This gives us huge flexibility in looking for solutions in the long and short term.

9. *Find out where the differences dovetail.* We have demonstrated that two people may want the same thing for very different reasons. It is usually this very difference which will enable us to find a practical solution. Dovetailing shows a respect for each other's integrity.

10. *Keep moving from positions to interests.* Sometimes we are unable to change our positions. Skilful questioning on the lines of 'what if...' often help. Ask what other solutions would work or ask them to think of any circumstances where their own solution might not apply. This encourages a reframe.

11. *Brainstorm the options.* Brainstorming can be a very useful tool for generating solutions. Sometimes the solution is obvious and at other times we may come across it by chance through creative thinking. In the case of the orange, for example, if both sisters had wanted the juice, perhaps we could have diluted it with water, or bought more oranges or found something else for one of them to drink.

When win/win seems impossible

Most of us can probably think of an example of this type of situation, e.g., two good applicants seeking the same promotion or a clash between two equally important events.

On the face of it, a situation may seem impossible to resolve to everyone's satisfaction. Someone is going to remain aggrieved. In such a situation, what can be done to improve your chances of resolving the matter without affecting relationships? The exercise in Table 4.3 will help you.

We are using a win/win *approach* and not necessarily achieving a win/win *solution.* Approaching a conflict situation with the win/win mindset, however, is more likely to give us a good quality solution. Demonstrating willingness and carefully exploring all available options may be all that is necessary for the other party(ies) to reciprocate. And the unexpected outcome may be that one of the parties involved realizes that they are being unreasonable and changes tack!

1. *Take a broader perspective.* When we are enmeshed in conflict,

it is easy to develop tunnel vision. The here and now becomes more important than the long term. We may agree to a solution offering long-term benefits at the expense of what looks like a short-term loss. It may also be useful to redefine what we mean by a win and look at what we can do to rebalance a loss.

2. *How do you initiate a win/win approach?* It is always useful to start with some sort of conversational opener on the lines of 'I want to find a solution that will be fair for both (all) of us'. It would take a very unreasonable person to object to the notion of fairness for all. Another approach could be 'Let's take a closer look at our needs and concerns here. What will it take to satisfy us both?'

3. *Your next step is to probe below the surface.* What is a stated need really masking? Is there a hidden concern? Ask ques-

---

Exercise

Table 4.3 Seemingly impossible win/win situations

	Situation 1	Situation 2
Think of two situations where win/win seems impossible		
Why does win/win seem impossible? List the obstacles?		
Moving towards a win/win, consider: a) How can the obstacles be removed? b) Can a win be redefined? c) What can rebalance a loss? d) What is the long-term perspective?		
What unexpected win/win outcome may conceivably occur?		

Source: Reprinted with permission from Fiona Hollier, Kerrie Murray and Helena Cornelius (1993) *Conflict Resolution Trainers Manual: 12 Skills*, Conflict Resolution Network, Australia, H13.

tions such as 'What's your real need here?' or 'Why does this seem like the best solution to you?'

4. *Ask 'What would it take to fix the problem?'* Remember that your objective is to try and work towards a solution that will satisfy you both. With the correct information, you can begin to move towards a solution. You also need to present your own side clearly and ensure that you have been heard.
5. *What if the other person will not cooperate?* In an ideal world, we would put our hands out to people in a gesture of genuine friendliness and cooperation and they would respond in the same way. Sadly, life is not like that. There will always be people who are awkward and who will try your patience. There is a useful model that demonstrates that behaviour breeds behaviour (Figure 4.3).

Returning to the coin activity I described earlier on. If we planted one person in the group to use a win/win approach and demonstrate, non-verbally, that both parties could win if they chose to cooperate, that partnership would swiftly start winning more points. If we carried on with the experiment for long enough, other partners would notice what was happening and, seeing the logic of it, quickly follow suit.

A common objection to win/win is 'Supposing I choose to be open and use win/win but the other person doesn't – then they will have the advantage over me and win the best deal. If I don't win the best deal, I'll lose my job.'

My response is that you can never 'lose' if you truly maintain a

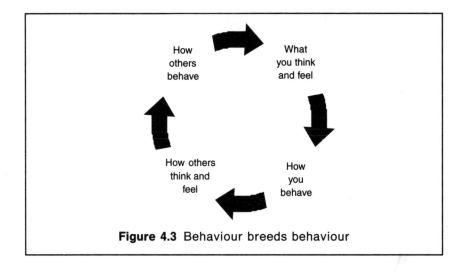

Figure 4.3 Behaviour breeds behaviour

win/win approach. Suppose the other person does take advantage of you and appears to 'win' a better deal in the short term. Your conscience is clear and you know that you were negotiating with a dishonourable person. And if that is the case, would you want to do business with that person? Do you see an advantage in being equally duplicitous? If so, then this book is probably not for you.

In general, if you maintain a calm, supportive win/win approach, you will encourage the other party. If you retaliate with a win/lose or by giving up, then you will achieve the very opposite. However, if you are in a conflict with someone who simply will not respond, then it is time to ask yourself whether the conflict is worth resolving or if you need a third party to mediate. We will return to this point later.

Summary

In this chapter, we considered intention behind behaviour. We examined different approaches involving win/lose types of behaviour and the physiological reason behind it. We explored the notion of needs before solutions and how to identify needs in order to take both sides into consideration when negotiating a solution. Finally, we discussed how behaviour breeds behaviour and that it only takes one person to change attitude for a win/win approach to occur.

5

Learning to respond

A great many people think they are thinking, when they are merely rearranging their prejudices.

(William James, 1842–1910, psychologist and philosopher)

Our values and beliefs influence our thoughts and our thoughts influence our behaviour. In this chapter we will learn how to take control of our thoughts and recognize when we are sending self-sabotage messages to ourselves. Once we have become more aware of our internal dialogues or 'mindchatter' then we can explore ways of using this to help us to respond appropriately, giving us the advantage in a conflict.

Do you ever find yourself losing control and saying what you do not mean when someone really annoys you? I call this the vending machine syndrome. Someone comes up to you, puts their pennies in your slot, presses your button and out comes the same reaction – time after time after time...

How would that person feel if they put in their money, confidently pressed the button which should deliver black coffee without sugar only to find that their cup contains sweetened cappuccino? They might wonder if they had pressed the wrong button or if the machine was in need of service. Vending machines, however, are not yet capable of a creative response – we are.

Why do some people react positively, others negatively to the same situation?

Heather's story

I dislike unplanned change. I don't like to be caught unaware. I even loathe surprises. If somebody organized a surprise birthday party for me, I would probably never forgive them. And yet my boyfriend thrives on change and impulse. He will decide what to do ten minutes before he does it. If a dozen friends dropped in unexpectedly for a meal, he would be in seventh heaven – even if his fridge contained nothing but half a pint of milk and some margarine!

To understand ourselves better, it is useful to ascertain where our 'programmes' come from. What makes us different? What colours our perceptions? The answers could include:

- age
- culture
- religion
- gender
- education
- background
- position in society
- job/career
- previous experience
- character
- nature/genes
- prevailing external influences/context.

Human beings are complex creatures. We are all individual and unique. We think differently, we speak differently and we behave differently. Our thoughts influence our behaviour. We are what we think. Henry Ford is believed to have said, 'If you think you can or you think you can't, you are right'. Therefore, to understand our behaviour in any given situation, we need to examine what is going on in our brains – our thought processes.

Our brains are divided into two hemispheres – the left hemisphere and the right hemisphere. New information and theories emerge daily, but for the purposes of this book, I continue to support the hypothesis that the two brain hemispheres each have their own distinct thinking pattern. The left side of the brain is the logical, sequential, detailed side, responsible for language, numerical skills, reasoning and scientific skills. The right brain is responsible for insight, imagination, and creativity. Knowing both sides of your brain is an important step in liberating your creative potential (Edwards, 1979).

It may be useful to approach problems using the dual-brain approach. If the problem appears to be one created by the right side of the brain – such as an overemotional response – then a left-brain approach may be helpful. If, on the other hand, the problem is a left sided one – a sequential, logical sort of problem – it can be useful to use our imagination to start us off in the right direction.

There are many instances of this: Einstein daydreaming about what it would be like to ride on a beam of light produced the relativity theory and Newton's research into gravitation started when an apple fell on his head. If we want a new and fresh approach to dealing with the problems life throws at us daily, it would be helpful to try on new thinking habits. There may be nothing at all wrong with the way you think right now but if you can identify common thinking patterns which impede your new approach, would not that be useful to you?

A great deal of research has gone into identifying common faulty thinking patterns, or cognitive distortions. Edward de Bono (1977) uses the following metaphor for thinking patterns. If we filled a shallow baking tray with jelly, and slowly poured boiling water into the middle, it would create an indentation. If we allowed this to overflow, it would create a channel. If we now pour another spoonful of water into the indentation the water will run along the channel that has already been created. If we continue to do this, the channel will become deeper each time.

We can see the same thing happening with our thinking. At a certain age, we may fall into our particular habit of faulty thinking. This forms a neural pathway. Next time we are faced with a similar situation, our thoughts find it easier to use the same neural pathway than to create new connections. And as we continue to think in that same old way, so we make the neural path stronger and more pronounced. It is so much easier to maintain old ways than it is to form new ones.

There has been a good deal of research into faulty thinking habits. Here are a few such habits based on those suggested by Schafer:

- *Bi-polar thinking*. You itemize in absolute categories. A film is either unmissable or totally unwatchable.
- *Overgeneralizing*. You generalize from one single event to all or most things. You misdiagnose a work problem, therefore, you are totally inept at your job.
- *Dwelling on the downside*. You dwell on negative aspects while screening out the positive. 'I have had nothing but trouble from this organization since the day I started.'
- *Awfulizing*. You turn a difficult situation into something ghastly. 'Today has been the worst day of my life – I missed the train and was late for my meeting.'
- *Doom and gloom thinking*. You always expect the very worst to happen or predict something will turn out badly. This is typified by the Victor Meldrew character in the popular television series, *One Foot In The Grave*.
- *'Everyone is out to get me' thinking*. You assume that people are reacting badly to you, or talking about you. Taken to extremes this behaviour can be paranoid.
- *Exaggerated thinking*. You overstate events. This could be either negative or positive. Either way, it is giving a false picture.
- *Shoulding and musting*. You constantly criticize yourself and others with 'shoulds' and 'should nots', 'musts', 'oughts' and 'have tos'.
- *But it is not fair*. You feel resentful because the world does not conform to what you consider to be fair.
- *I am responsible*. You believe that everything is your fault. You imagine that others' behaviour or feelings is somehow tied up to something you said or did.
- *Thou shalt always find a third party to blame*. Constantly blaming others/circumstances when events go wrong, not accepting responsibility for the ways in which you may have contributed to the problem.
- *Having to be right*. Being proved wrong is the worst thing in the world that could happen to you. To lose face would destroy your self-worth. You go out of your way to have the last word.
- *Perfectionism*. You indulge in self-sabotage by imposing impossibly high standards on yourself and others. You prefer to take no action at all rather than do something less than perfect. This thinking is often linked to procrastination.

Source: Adapted from *Stress Management for Wellness* by Walt Schafer (1987).

How many of the above thinking patterns apply to you? How many do you recognize in others? Do any of them particularly incense you?

How might this work in practice? Picture somebody whose usual approach is to consider only the downside. Can you imagine how differently this person may approach problems, conflicts and stresses from someone who considers the positive side? Each of the above thinking distortions will produce someone with a distinctly characteristic way of behaving and handling life.

Gail's story

> My parents were always very proud of my academic record and achievements, and used to boast about me to their friends. They had very high expectations of me and I started to worry that I might let them down. I became a perfectionist myself and ended up stressed and worried. I would rewrite reports endlessly, sending back letters for retyping if there was even one minuscule error. I was unable to delegate to anyone because I could always do things better and then I would procrastinate over doing it myself in case it wasn't perfect. I never noticed how I had undermined my staff and caused them to resent me. Then I was taken to hospital with a gallstone and was forced to take time off work. When I got back, I discovered that, not only had my deputy manager got the department running like clockwork, but that I had never seen the staff working so industriously and enthusiastically. I had a heart to heart with my deputy and invited her to give me honest feedback. I worked very hard on myself since then and can honestly say it has made a huge difference to my personal and working life.

Reaction versus response

In common parlance reacting and responding have become almost interchangeable. In the last chapter, we examined the difference between the two.

To react is similar to the knee-jerk we normally exhibit when a doctor taps our knee with an instrument. It is one of the simplest parts of the human nervous system. In conflict, we may react in an emotional, impulsive manner. To respond, however, is to give the stimulus some thought and then offer the response in a considered manner. To react is to listen to ourselves, whereas to respond is to listen to others.

Exercise

In your workbook, list three incidents where you reacted to an outside stimulus without thinking it through.

Now list three incidents where you responded by carefully weighing up what was said and considering your thinking or behavioural response.

In what way did the two differ? Did the other party react or respond according to how you behaved? Did your thought patterns influence whether you reacted or responded? What lessons might be learned from this activity? Remember:

My body may react but I can still choose to respond.

Our thoughts and our mindchatter

Exercise

Try this. Close the book; put it to one side for 60 seconds then reopen it at this page.

Did you hear a voice in your head talking to you? Do you remember much of what it said? You might have heard: 'This is strange. Why am I closing the book? Am I meant to time myself? If so, why didn't she say make sure you have a watch? What a silly waste of time.' This is known as your mindchatter or your internal commentator and it can be your friend or your enemy. The choice is yours.

So, what was your mindchatter saying? Was it telling you that this was a waste of time and perhaps you would be better occupied by ignoring the instructions and carrying on with your reading? Or was it saying 'This is fun. I wonder what will happen now? I always enjoy this type of activity.' Can you see that the one will put you in an impatient and negative frame of mind while the other will leave you with a sense of anticipation and curiosity?

Can you change a negative internal running commentary? You certainly can with perseverance. No one ever achieved a flat stomach with one sit-up! First, listen carefully to what the commentary is saying. Now form a mental picture of the type of person that would speak like that. Imagine them in every detail – are they old or young? Male or female? Fun or boring? Successful or not? Friend or enemy? Now imagine that person sitting inside your head, observing the world through your eyes and then telling you what to do and what not to do, constantly criticizing you for this and for that, opinionated, envious and practically running your life for you. Surely not!

If this person were real and followed you around all the time, you would surely lose patience and tell them to go away. And yet most of us spend our lives under the tyranny of this internal commentator and never give it a thought.

Do yourself a favour. Next time it interferes with the way you want to run your life – tell it to go away. Reword the comments positively and repeat them to yourself a few times. For example, if somebody contradicts you aggressively at a meeting, and your inner commentator starts goading you with words like, 'How dare they question my judgement, I am absolutely right and I won't be humiliated in public', change it to 'That's interesting. They are probably having a bad day and haven't thought their opinion through. I won't be drawn into this'.

Exercise

Review the three incidents in which you reacted impulsively and the commentary you were listening to. Explore ways of making the commentary more constructive.

The power of positive language

Never underestimate the power of a word. Words can make you ill or well. Happy or sad, violent or submissive, A word can produce biochemical changes in your body, just as a drug can. This is how hypnosis and hypnotherapy work.

It is said that the Inuit people have approximately 14 different words for the concept of 'snow'. The question is, do they regard snow in a different way? Do they literally see 14 different types of snow? I believe the answer to be 'Yes'.

If we use our language as a tool, we can help change our attitude to the world and to others, as well as changing our emotional reactions to events. The average English speaker uses only a fraction of the English vocabulary available to us. If you use a limited vocabulary, you are also limiting your emotional experiences and denying yourself the opportunity to grow and develop.

We make sense of our experiences by labelling them with words. If we habitually use words like 'furious', 'livid', 'mad' or 'really gets up my nose', these words will shape our experiences and we will actually display furious, livid or mad behaviour when we could have chosen to be 'bothered' or 'irritated'.

How often do you use the word 'hate' when a less emotionally charged word would have conveyed a more accurate emotion? Do you 'hate' your nose or 'hate' your hair? Do you 'hate' your boss or 'hate' Joan in accounts? You may not like them very much, you may even find them difficult to associate with, but it is unlikely that you 'hate' them. Hate should be handled carefully and, if it needs to be used at all, should be used wisely and not dispensed like confetti.

Another example is the word 'argument'. If we think of it as an informed debate or a dialogue, we take away the sting and concentrate on the positive aspects of it. In fact, we welcome a dialogue or a debate but we try to avoid arguments.

Anthony Robbins (1992) calls the power of the word 'transformational vocabulary' and recounts a study conducted in a prison. The researchers found that many inmates were incapable of expressing their emotions with the appropriate words. The only way they could communicate was with physical action. Their limited vocabulary also limited their emotional range of expression. This led them to react to the slightest feelings of discomfort by channelling them into violence.

Begin to be aware of the vocabulary people around you use to express their emotions. Many people, especially the younger socially disadvantaged ones, have such a limited vocabulary that they use four-letter words to express everything from anger to excitement. When faced with an emotion that they are unable to name or label, you can see the momentary confusion fleet across their faces and in microseconds they react aggressively. It is not that they are stupid – they are simply making the best choice they can with the limited resources at their disposal.

There is also a cultural aspect to the emotional range of language that we use. Shelle Rose Charvet (1997) argues that some cultures use superlatives as the usual way of speaking while others avoid them as much as possible. As a Middle-Eastern, where we tend to exaggerate feelings and events, I have to be constantly vigilant and use less theatrical language in the West.

The narrow range of our language is probably responsible for the stereotypical stiff upper-lipped British image. Charvet's research demonstrates that while Americans will use vocabulary that veers from one extreme to the other – 'A complete disaster' to 'amazingly wonderful' – the English (particularly the upper class) will use a range of 'Not too good' to 'Not too bad'. Notice how many Americans will listen to over-the-top hype, while the British will cringe in embarrassment.

Our responses also help our emotional states. For example, in the United Kingdom, a common response to 'How are you?' is 'Not too bad'. In Canada, it might be 'Pretty good' and in the USA 'Great'. Which of the above responses is likely to put you in a positive frame of mind to tackle your day?

Exercise

Note in your workbook the words you habitually use to express a negative emotion, and use an alternative 'softer' word, e.g.:

Hard expression	*Soft expression*
Stressed	Challenged
Miserable	Ready to be cheered up
Furious	Intense

Now identify the words you habitually use to express positive emotion and choose a more energetic alternative:

Bland expression	*Energetic expression*
OK	Couldn't be better
Not bad	Really good
Happy	Tremendous

Give yourself a gift and make friends with your thesaurus. Set yourself the challenge of learning at least one new word a day and have fun using them.

Thomas Crum (1987) presents the Perfection vs Discovery model for understanding how our thinking can affect our behaviour, which I interpret as in Figures 5.1 and 5.2.

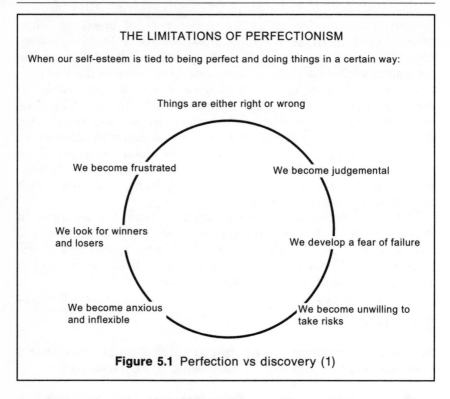

Figure 5.1 Perfection vs discovery (1)

Looking for the learning in conflict

Part of the creative response is to ask yourself what you can learn from any occurrence. One of my favourite expressions is 'What is the universe trying to tell me?' This helps you to find something positive in every experience. Learning does not just happen by chance. We need to seize every opportunity to extract something new and useful from it.

Another way of assessing events creatively is reframing. For example, when job-hunting, sure as night follows day, rejections will follow applications. As a rough guide, expect 19 rejections before being invited to an interview. Why not celebrate each rejection as it arrives? Instead of a sinking heart, we could think 'Great! That's one more towards my target of 20 and one nearer an interview'. I have used this technique and it works.

Choosing a creative response means looking for the opportunity in conflict – changing problems into challenges as we saw with the use of transformational vocabulary. It also allows us to shift from fixed positions and to seek more options that just might satisfy more of the involved parties' needs and concerns.

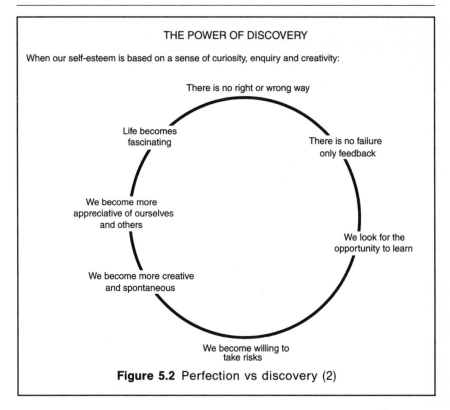

THE POWER OF DISCOVERY

When our self-esteem is based on a sense of curiosity, enquiry and creativity:

There is no right or wrong way

Life becomes
fascinating

There is no failure
only feedback

We become more
appreciative of ourselves
and others

We look for the
opportunity to learn

We become more creative
and spontaneous

We become willing to
take risks

Figure 5.2 Perfection vs discovery (2)

After all, you have spent your time and money reading this chapter, would it not be a pity if you were not given the live opportunity to practise your new style thinking skills?

Summary

In this chapter we explored our thoughts and how they influence our behaviour. Faulty thinking patterns are very common and are one of the main contributors to stress as well as our attitudes and our behaviours. We discussed some of the main types of faulty thinking patterns and asked you to identify your own. We then examined the difference between reaction and response and how to take control of our 'internal commentator'. We also considered how our vocabulary influences our thoughts and the effect of using appropriate vocabulary to enhance responses or tone down reactions.

6

Creating empathy

Amazing things happen when you make people feel they are valued as individuals.

(Herb Kelleher, airline executive)

One of the principles of resolving conflict is to establish empathy or rapport with the other party. The more we know and understand others, the less we fear them; the more we can find out about what makes them tick and why they say and do the things they do, the more we can accept their points of view, even if they differ from our own. Its easy to have empathy with people we like, but how can we truly empathize with people we actually do not like very much or whose opinions are at the opposite ends of the scale to our own?

What is empathy?

The *Pocket Oxford Dictionary* defines empathy as 'the power of identifying oneself mentally with (and so fully comprehending) the person or object of contemplation'.

Fisher, Kopelman and Schneider (1994) recount the story of a US Army colonel during the Vietnam war. He questioned the desirability of considering a conflict from the point of view of one's adversaries. He maintained that to understand how others saw things might cause us to question the merits of our actions.

'The better we understand their concerns and their ideas,' he said, 'the greater the chance that we will lose confidence in the rightness of our own cause.'

When we listen to, and understand, many different points of view, we put our own into perspective. It does not mean that we will necessarily change our minds, in fact, what we hear may well reinforce our own points of view, but we will be doing so from a higher vantage point.

So often people confuse 'understanding' and 'agreeing with' another's point of view. We do not have to agree with another's point of view, but we do need to understand what it is they believe, what led them to believe that and the benefits they receive from retaining this belief. This gives you an advantage in any conflict.

Without communication there is no chance of resolving conflict. Take the general opinion that we should never communicate with terrorists unless they change their ways and abandon their activities. At an emotional level, I am sure there are few who would disagree. But at a rational level, what chance is there of any terrorists abandoning their weapons without some form of communication?

To communicate effectively, we need to establish empathy. Another word for this is 'rapport' and I use the two interchangeably. We do not have to like the other party, but we do need to understand them. And doing so requires excellent communication skills, which can be learned.

My two presuppositions are that, first, each of us is an individual with our own history, values, culture, map of the world and carrying our own unique emotional baggage and, second, no two people, even twins, are exactly alike, or understand matters in exactly the same way.

The Torah says 'We see things not as they are, but as we are'. We colour other people's words and sentences with our own emotional crayons and then react to them as if they were fact.

How do we know when we are in empathy with another person? Look around you in a restaurant, airport lounge or wherever you enjoy people-watching. Notice that you instinctively can tell if a couple or a group have 'clicked'. What are the behavioural clues?

If two people are in rapport, they will unconsciously mirror each other's body language in some way. They will lean forward together or backwards together, they will look each other in the eye and will appear interested – they may smile more – or they may both look serious at the same time, instinctively mirroring each other's facial expressions. If we were near enough to hear their conversation, we would notice how their vocal tone, volume and rhythm were matching. If we observed even closer we would notice how their breathing was starting to synchronize. All this happens, and is observed, at an unconscious level.

The same process occurs in a group. Watch any group and you will begin to notice which members of the group are in tune with each other and which are not. Notice the inclusion and exclusion signals.

We create empathy by giving our undivided attention to the other party and by actively listening. This means *really* listening to what that person is saying, without giving advice or expressing our own opinion. Often we are so busy thinking of our reply that we miss what the person is saying.

If instead of reading this paragraph, I were standing in front of you and talking it through with you, my communication would be transmitted to you via three channels often referred to as the three Vs: Visual or body language, Vocal or voice, and Verbal or the words I use.

Research appears to confirm that in the event of an incongruent message, i.e. where verbal and non-verbal messages tell different stories, 93 per cent of the population would read the non-verbal elements (voice and body language), while only 7 per cent of the population would rely solely on the words (Charvet, 1997; Mehrabian, 1971).

You have probably noticed this for yourself. Say, you felt something was wrong with a colleague and on enquiring, he or she looks up, gives a watery smile and says 'No, no, I'm fine, honestly'. You would know, would you not?

We can create empathy both verbally and non-verbally.

Non-verbal empathy

The two main sets of non-verbal skills we can use to establish empathy are mirroring and matching, and pacing and leading. These techniques need to be used with great skill and subtlety otherwise the other person may feel you are mimicking them. Therefore, the first skill to hone is observation – using all of your senses to notice other people's body movements, gestures, poses and natural rhythms. Comedians are very good at this, putting their skills to a different use – copying and exaggerating people's gestures to make us laugh.

You can learn to do the same and then use some of the person's own movements very subtly to send the message 'we are very much alike'. When we first meet someone and make tentative steps to establish rapport by small talk, we first try to establish common ground – interests we share in common. Mirroring is a non-verbal version of the same principle.

We can mirror or match two main areas: body posture and tone of voice. If you are in rapport with somebody, you will mirror posture instinctively. The trick here is to match body posture with somebody you may not know very well or you may not particularly like. First observe posture: is the person standing/sitting in a fairly relaxed open manner or is there some tension there and perhaps folded arms? Are they sitting well back and straight up in their chair or are they more relaxed? Are their legs crossed or uncrossed?

Having observed posture, find a low-risk area where you can experiment with matching body posture. A good place to try is at a party or a pub, perhaps. Start to match body posture ever so subtly. One simple movement at a time until you feel more confident.

The other skill we use instinctively when we are establishing empathy is matching voice. If two people have mismatching voices, i.e. one has a high-pitched loud voice and the other is softly spoken, notice how they both move towards the middle range once they have established empathy. The softer-spoken person will raise their voice slightly and the higher-voiced person will lower his or hers.

People also speak at different speeds or tempo. When in conversation they will adjust their tempo to minimize the difference. Have you noticed how you automatically use the same rhythm and often words when speaking to someone who is not a native speaker of your language? A colleague of mine says she speaks two types of English: the one she uses at home with her family and friends, and the one she speaks when she goes to the Continent on business.

Matching voice tonality, tempo and rhythm, and using the same words as the other person will dramatically increase your chances of establishing a good working relationship with that person. Voice-matching skill training is a vital tool in all telesales environments.

Very advanced communicators also match body movements and rhythms, and even breathing. However, it is advisable to learn such advanced techniques in a training environment with a skilled instructor.

Once you have learned to mirror and match successfully, you can move on to the next stage, which is pacing and leading. Practice this a few times in low-risk situations until you feel comfortable with it.

If someone is shouting, and you remain calm, speaking in low, soft tones you are more likely to inflame the angry person than to calm them down. An angry person may interpret such a mismatch as non-caring on your part. On the other hand, if you match their anger, the conflict may become worse. The secret is to match their energy. Speak in a slightly louder and more energetic voice, increase your tempo and put your body into a state of 'relaxed alertness'. Once you have the other person's attention, you can reduce the conflict by lowering your voice gradually and decreasing the tempo. The other person will normally lower their voice to match your own. Finally, you may want to lead the person to a chair where you can both sit down and continue from there.

Pacing and leading alone can often be enough to calm a potentially explosive situation and are skills well worth practising.

Verbal empathy

What do people do when they first meet? They try to find common ground. Notice how we listen for clues that we can build on. The more you have in common with another person, the less likely it is that you will disagree with them. Actively seek commonality with others and you will be amazed at the difference it makes to the quality of your relationships.

If you frequently find yourself distracted when listening or if you suddenly come to the guilty realization that you missed the last few moments of conversation, you are not alone. We hear and absorb words much faster than we articulate them. When someone is talking to you – and particularly if that person speaks slowly – your brain has absorbed the drift and is busily trying to think of some way to keep itself occupied while the speaker is still finishing the sentence.

We do not always listen as attentively as we should. Life moves at a fast pace and there are so many other matters clamouring for our attention. In conversation, we are often mentally rehearsing our reply rather than concentrating on the message. We know when we are being listened to and we know when someone is only going through the motions.

There are many reasons these days that make listening more difficult. We are used to 'soundbites', commercial breaks, strong visuals. Everything moves at a much faster pace. Many children grow up nowadays without books. Instead they surf the net, and this encourages them to jump from one page to the next, following first one subject then another. Like a butterfly, we dip in and out and flutter off to another subject or another line of enquiry.

Much the same happens when we are talking. What passes for conversation these days is often no more than simultaneous monologues. Real dialogue is a remnant of the past. And so we do not hear each other's points of view, so wrapped up are we in delivering our own.

Many of us inadvertently alienate people in our daily conversation by using certain phrases. To understand why these responses can produce such a negative result, imagine someone using them on you. Only an insensitive person, or somebody who was not listening to you anyway, would carry right on talking.

The effect of these responses on the other person can be profound. People have expressed anger, loss of self-esteem, resentment, feeling snubbed, disrespected and belittled. It is amazing how a few words from one person can produce such intense feelings in another.

Here are some responses to use with great caution when you are trying to foster good relationships with others. In football, when a player has committed a 'foul' the referee may hold up a red card. Here are some verbal fouls that merit a red card. They are based on those identified by Robert Bolton (1979) and Hollier, Murray and Cornelius (1993). How many of them do you recognize?

1. *Criticizing*. We often do not realize how judgemental we are being. Sometimes, we criticize out of a misguided notion that we are being helpful or giving constructive feedback.
   Example: 'I'm not surprised you mislaid that article. I don't know how you ever find anything on that desk of yours anyway.'
2. *Labelling*. Another destructive habit. We often use words such as 'empire builder', 'prima donna', 'moaning Minnie', 'office Casanova', 'bimbo' and so on. These can be very insulting to another, even if they are said jokingly.
   Examples: 'That's a typical woman's remark'; 'Only a man could be so insensitive'.
3. *Diagnosing*. Playing amateur psychologist is another irritating trick. One sure way to stop a conversation is to tell somebody that they have a complex about something or are 'in denial' or use other such terms which are in vogue.
   Examples: 'It sounds as if that's an ingrained childhood response'; 'You're playing the victim card again'.

4. *Manipulative praising*. We often use praise to achieve results so it is not surprising that we think, 'I wonder what they're after'. Praise can suggest that the praiser is somehow superior to the person they are praising. This can make people feel uncomfortable. Use praise with care otherwise it rebounds.

Example: 'You're so good with numbers, I'd like you to compile the sales statistics.'

5. *Ordering*. No one likes being told what to do. Some cultures, such as the military or the police, use ordering as part of their normal conversation but they rarely work in everyday interaction. Office bullies often rely on ordering and threatening to get their way.

Examples: 'I want that done and I want it done now'; 'There's to be no discussion of this. I've already made the decision'.

6. *Threatening*. This produces the same results as ordering – defiance, resentment and, possibly, disobedience. Most people can achieve their outcomes without having to resort to threats; however, we may still use threatening language unthinkingly.

Examples: 'You'd better improve your performance before next month's appraisals'; 'If those sales figures of yours don't improve, you're the next for the chop'.

7. *Moralizing*. If you want to be unpopular, pepper your conversation liberally with 'You should/shouldn't/ought/oughtn't...' Nobody likes being preached to and the common response is 'You're not my mother'. Sometimes, the moralizing is implied but it is still just as annoying, for example, 'I don't know how anyone manages without a computer these days' the implication being 'you should get yourself a computer'.

Examples: 'You shouldn't take things so seriously'; 'You really ought to give more thought to your future security'.

8. *Interrogating*. Used effectively, questions can be a prized communication skill. They help the other person to clarify their own thoughts. However, interrogating is more appropriate to the police station or the law courts. Questions can be welcomed as showing interest or resented as being intrusive. Both the content of our questions and our tone of voice make the difference.

Examples: 'Exactly what did you say to him?' 'Where were you when this happened?' 'How do you know – were you there?'

9. *Advising*. If people want advice they will normally ask for it. If they do not, then do not give it. Giving people advice can belittle them or patronize them. We often want to air an issue or to talk through a problem to clarify our own thoughts, even though we know what needs to be done. Advising can also be quite insulting to another. The hidden message is 'the solution to your problem is quite obvious to me. You must be very dim not to see it'.

   Examples: 'Well, if I were you, I would...'; 'Have you thought of...?'; 'Why don't you just...?'

10. *Topping*. This is so common that most people think it is an empathy builder! No sooner do you start telling someone about your awful journey than they regale you with how much worse theirs was. In fact, there is a good, but misguided, intention there to say 'I know how you feel, I share this with you'. Still, the net result is that the focus of attention has been moved from you to them. They have cut you off in mid-air and are not interested in what you have to say.

    Example: 'I had a bad cold over the weekend.'

    'Isn't that strange. I was really quite ill myself. I had to make an emergency call. What a rigmarole. Let me tell you what happened...'

11. *Reassurance*. If someone trusts you enough to say 'I feel like a complete failure', the last thing they want to hear from you is 'Of course, you're not'. That is such a glib response that it is likely to leave the speaker feeling that you have missed the point or are not interested. A better response would be 'You sound demoralized. Do you want to talk about it?'

    Examples: 'It'll all blow over – just forget it'; 'It's probably a five-minute wonder'.

You may know other examples of verbal fouls that are conversation stoppers. You may have been on the receiving end, or you may have used them yourself. Sometimes, of course, you can use these to your advantage if you really are trying to put a person off or cut short an unwelcome conversation. But there are other kinder and more tactful ways to do so.

We need to recognize the phrases we use which may inadvertently be creating barriers in our communication; however, we should not worry about them so much that we become self-conscious about every sentence we utter. We all use these phrases in our conversation from time to time and most of our relationships can survive the damage.

What is the difference between hearing and active listening? Active listening means putting someone else's needs before our own – focusing all your attention on the speaker and listening for the meaning behind the words. It also means ensuring the other person knows you are really listening by nodding and using encouraging phrases appropriately.

Skilful questioning also encourages communication. There are two main types: open and closed.

1. Closed questions can be answered with a simple 'Yes' or 'No'. Use them to verify information or confirm understanding, agreement or commitment or choose between two alternatives. Such questions are not really suited to active listening. As their name implies, they close down a conversation.
2. Open questions are designed to provoke thought and elicit an extended response. This is why they are so vital to active listening. Use them to encourage free thinking, facilitate feedback, create involvement and commitment, and establish empathy.

A colleague recently shared the following model (Figure 6.1) with me. She calls it the 'six bottoms sitting on a fence'. They represent the seven question openers: 'What', 'Why', 'Where', 'When', 'Which', 'Who' or 'How' (six Ws and one H).

The following are some of the types of open questions you can use in conversation:

1. *Reflective questions.* These are very useful as a means of clarification and rephrasing. Using a reflective question will help the speaker focus on what they have said and possibly expand on it. 'Let me make sure I have understood this correctly ... is that what you meant?'
2. *Justifying/challenging questions.* These questions need to be put in a non-confrontational manner otherwise they defeat the purpose. They are useful in helping the other person to examine their own feelings, attitudes or reasons. 'You say ...

Figure 6.1 Six bottoms on a fence

how can you be sure?' or 'When you say ... what do you think is behind it? Or 'What leads you to...?'

3. *Hypothetical questions.* Use when introducing a new idea or concept. They are very powerful in coaching, counselling, problem-solving and interviewing. They can help the other person step outside the situation and see it from another angle. 'What if...?' or 'Suppose we were unable to...?'. 'What would happen if we...?' 'What's the worst that could happen if...?

4. *Probing questions.* These need a high degree of skill to use otherwise we find ourselves interrogating, which is one of our verbal fouls. Use probing questions when the respondent is unable or unwilling to give a fuller answer by mixing open, closed, reflective, challenging and hypothetical questions. Probing should be carried out with tact, patience and persistence.

Active listening

When I introduce this concept in communication workshops, participants often say that it is likely to make them more self-conscious and less relaxed in conversation: 'If I have to choose my words so carefully, I won't have time to listen'; 'People should accept me for what I am. I speak my mind'; 'It's unrealistic. If I tried that in the pub, my mates would think I'd gone mad!'

Active listening is not something you do all the time. Used appropriately, it is a communication and management skill. It is not intended to replace friendly banter, lively after-dinner conversations and animated discussion. But used in the right setting and for the appropriate purpose, it can help the speaker identify and resolve their own problems and it can build trust, loyalty and friendship.

Exercise

Think back to the last time you had a conversation with someone who was really listening to you. If you have difficulty remembering an occasion, that probably proves the point that very few people practise this vital skill. If you can identify such an occasion, note down what the other person was doing and compare it with the following principles of best practice.

1. Active listening works best in a quiet, comfortable and private environment. There should be no barriers, in the form of tables or desks, between you and the other person. Try to ensure that the chairs are also of equal status and height.
2. Place your entire attention on the speaker and avoid talking about yourself.
3. Repeat the gist of what the speaker is saying, in your own words, to check your understanding.
4. Feed back feelings, 'It sounds as though you were hurt/felt left out...'
5. Probe gently if you feel it is appropriate, i.e. 'So how did that make you feel/How do you plan to deal with that?'
6. Reflect back so that the speaker can hear and understand his or her own meaning. This helps the person clarify his or her own thoughts.
7. Help the other person reframe negative emotions or attitudes. 'There is no way out of this' could elicit a response of 'You can't see a way out of this right now?'
8. Do not be embarrassed by silences. These are essential to allow you time to think and reflect.
9. Remain alert to physical changes, i.e. reddening eyes, clenched jaw, closed fists trembling, which could indicate a rise in feelings.
10. Notice that people shift body positions in response to changes in thoughts or emotions. Wait till they have settled into their new position and then try asking how they feel about things now.
11. Even well-intentioned comments can be badly received sometimes. Avoid the verbal fouls discussed earlier. Even if they do not shut down the conversation immediately, you will notice a change in the energy and a reluctance to carry on.
12. Pay close attention to body language and practise your mirroring skills.

Because life is so competitive, we often feel we have got to put our point of view across first. We are used to 'they who shout loudest are served fastest' and we are anxious to defend our positions, interests and self-esteem by being right. In active listening, we must put the other person first.

This may seem as if we are unnecessarily complicating what should be a natural response – listening. In fact, we have lost the art of listening naturally and often find we have to relearn the skill.

Challenging

If used appropriately, challenging the other party can be another invaluable tool to help them clarify their own thinking and resolve problems. In NLP terms this is called the precision model.

Our words can never keep pace with our thoughts. For our thoughts to be delivered in a neatly packaged sentence, we constantly find ourselves generalizing, distorting and deleting

This often makes it hard for the listener to understand the deeper meaning of the communication. To find out precisely what the other person wants to say, we need to use a series of questions or challenges. Here are a few examples of how the technique is used:

1. *Vague statements*
   To challenge ask who, what, which, how ... specifically?
   Statement: *I don't understand.*
   Response: *What specifically don't you understand?*
2. *Generalizations*
   Words like every, each, all, none, never, no one etc. The skill is to get the speaker to voice an exception.
   Statement: *Nobody has any time for me.*
   Response: *Does anyone ever have any time for you?* or *Nobody?*
3. *Comparisons*
   Words like more, less, better, worse. Your task is to discover what their point of comparison is.
   Statement: *I think he is worse than he was.*
   Response: *Worse than what?* or *How much worse?*
4. *Shoulding/musting*
   Words like must, need, should, have to, ought to. Ask 'What makes it necessary?' or 'What would happen if... ?'
   Statement: *I have to come out on top all the time.*
   Challenge: *What makes that necessary?* or *What would happen if you didn't?*
5. *Negativity*
   Words like can't, impossible, never.
   Respond by asking: 'What prevents... ?' or 'What would happen if... ?'
   Statement: *I simply can't relax.*
   Response: *What stops you relaxing?* or *What would happen if you did relax?*

Caution: Great care must be taken not to make your discussion sound like a third-degree interrogation. Probing empathetically will help you detect inaccuracies in speech and improve your own communication. Make sure you pay attention to your voice and inflection so that you sound interested and friendly. You can also soften the questions with phrases such as 'I'm interested as to why...' or 'I'm curious to find out...'.

Before expressing an opinion ask yourself the following questions:

- Am I sure of my facts?
- Is what I want to say worth saying?
- If it is, does the other person want to hear it?
- If so, is this the appropriate moment to say it?

> *The meaning of my communication is the response I get.*

Understanding different communication styles

If we want to put ourselves in the other person's shoes, a useful starting-point is to acknowledge that we each have our own communication and behavioural styles. If we can learn to value the strengths of each style and to tolerate the shortcomings, we can dramatically improve our communication. With time and practice, we can quickly learn to identify a person's tendencies and adapt our own responses accordingly. This does not mean disguising our own natural response or attempting to be what we are not. It is simply a skill for creating empathy and being flexible in our own responses.

There are many different models available for behavioural and communication styles. Indeed, they have existed for centuries. Hippocrates was one of the first to write about these, believing that our bodies contained four fundamental humours, based on the four elements of fire, air, water and earth. Our personalities and moods depended on which of the four was dominant.

Since then there have been many modern theories of personality based on the four-elements theory. Carl Jung (1851–1961) worked extensively with this theory. Many of the psychometric tests used for job interviews are based on this. While it may be trite to reduce our rich, complex and individual personalities to only four categories, strangely enough, it works. Valuing our different strengths and adapting to each other's shortcomings is a vital component of creating empathy.

The following case study serves as a good introduction.

> Chris, Tom, Kim and Nizar, are four divisional team managers and members of the relocation steering committee. They are meeting to discuss an imminent reorganization of their divisions. The changes will include a move to offices down the road, six redundancies and a new software system. Let us see if you can recognize the four broad categories from the following descriptions:

- Chris is keen on the change. She knows which members of her department are to be made redundant and is resigned to the inevitable upsets that are about to happen. She thinks they will be quickly forgotten, particularly as the changes will make the company much more competitive and leading edge. She wants the move to take place as soon as possible and has put herself forward as chair of the relocation steering committee. At meetings, she does not hesitate to express her opinions or disagree with those expressing a different point of view. She can sometimes be tactless but does achieve results. She likes being involved in the big picture and prefers to delegate the tiresome details to others. She is very goal oriented and has set herself a three-year target to achieve a directorship.
- Tom is in his element. Change always excites him and he considers this his opportunity to introduce a feng shui consultant, whom he met at a networking evening, to make the new premises brighter and friendlier to work in. He is very sorry to see some of his colleagues being made redundant and has made sure everyone knows his opinion. He knows everyone in the office and is frequently seen in the pub across the road having a drink and a chat after work. He thinks the change is for the good, though, and is determined to do his bit to keep morale high. He is working on a new incentive scheme that he intends to introduce once his team has moved, to keep them happy and motivated. Meetings are always much more fun with Tom there. He keeps up the banter and seems to have an endless stream of creative ideas, but he becomes bored very quickly and prefers someone else to deal with the actual nitty-gritty.
- Kim is very upset about the imminent changes. She does not see why anyone should be made redundant and would be

more willing to discuss an across the board pay cut for everyone in order to cling on to her staff. She is concerned with the details of the move and to ensure that there is minimum disruption to the people concerned. She has been to the new office to ensure that everyone there has enough space and will be comfortable. Two years ago she went on an evening counselling course and has turned into the unofficial office agony aunt. She is very loyal to the company and to her team. She is scrupulously fair and always sees issues from both sides. She has been cajoled into joining the relocation committee although she does not like committees, which tend to become too argumentative for her liking. For some reason, she has also been nominated to take the minutes – this is a real chore taking up even more of her time, but she does not like to let down her colleagues.

- Nizar has been immersed in paperwork since the move was first mooted. He has been nominated to coordinate the tenders for the new software system, as well as the quotations for the actual move. Being very thorough, he goes through each piece of paper with a fine-toothed comb. Nothing escapes his notice and he will phone to query many of the details. Although he is, of course, very sorry to see some of his colleagues go, he is more concerned with completing the work and the reallocation of duties and responsibilities. The office filing system is to be converted to microfiche and he has spent many sleepless nights worrying about the possibility of errors or files going missing. He has been working overtime because he cannot trust anyone else to do the job as thoroughly as he can.

You may recognize these four categories of behavioural style (see Table 6.1). You probably know instinctively which one is the most like you. The four dominant styles are based on two continua: contemplative to expressive, and task focused to people focused.

1. Contemplatives or introverts may be less assertive while expressives or extraverts may be more assertive.
2. Task focused may be less responsive to others and people focused may be more responsive.

Each quadrant in Figure 6.2 shows its own behavioural characteristics. Some we may regard as strengths and others as shortcomings. Most behaviours are in any case on a continuum, with

Table 6.1 Four behavioural styles

People who behave like Chris may be:	*People who behave like Kim may be:*
Expressive and confident	Reserved and observant
Decisive, like to take action	Good team workers
A challenge to authority	Tolerant and patient
Keen to take the lead	Put upon, find difficulty in saying 'No'
Highly competitive	Think of other people before
Tactless or insensitive	themselves
Often impatient	Loyal and trustworthy
Big-picture people, prefer delegating	Easily upset – fragile confidence
details	Holistic in approach
Over-optimistic – often overlook	Attentive to detail
drawbacks in projects	Perceptive and considerate of others'
Keen to promote change	feelings
	Suspicious of sudden changes

People who behave like Tom may be:	*People who behave like Nizar may be:*
Outgoing and friendly	Reserved and deliberate
Enthusiastic and charismatic	Systematic and methodical
Entertaining, with sense of humour	Inflexible, working by the book
Impulsive	Detailed, concentrate on minutiae
Creative, sometimes unrealistic	Critical – concentrate on what could
Big picture people – details bore them	go wrong
Carried away with plans, caught out	Uncomfortable with multi-tasking
when things go wrong	Perfectionists – do not like delegating
Welcome change	Prefer to plan for change, good at
	contingencies

degrees of extremity. Taken to excess they shift from being strengths to weaknesses.

Each of us is made up of these four behavioural types, mixed in different proportions. How we behave at any time may well be context dependent. For example, we may act like Chris at work and Kim at home, or vice versa. If our behaviours were colours, we would come in all shades from the palest of pastels to the deepest of hues. Most of us also have a natural style and an adapted one. Our adapted style depends on how self-aware we are. If we notice that we have the shortcomings of one type, we may try to compensate by taking on some characteristics of another and so on.

What is the importance of understanding different behavioural types in conflict? When we are in conflict with each other, we tend to see ourselves as right and, consequently, others as wrong. The Tao te Ching says:

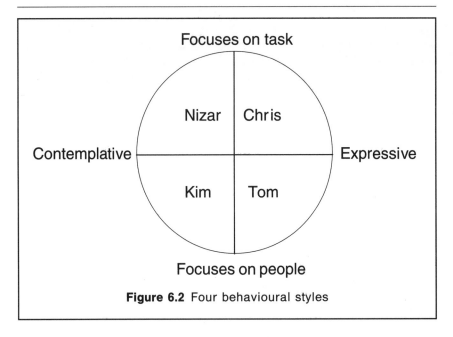

Figure 6.2 Four behavioural styles

When people see things as beautiful,
Other things become ugly.
When people see some things as good,
Other things become bad.

If we can learn to value differences and other people's strengths while tolerating and compensating for their short-comings, then will we move on to another plane of communication. People pay attention to different things. While we may concentrate on one aspect of a problem, they are concentrating on another. On our way to work in the morning, do we pay attention to the noise and pollution or to the trees and birdsong? Once we begin to welcome other people's diverse opinions as a forum for learning and as an opportunity for dialogue, warmth and understanding, we can truly say that we have entered into the conflict-resolving mindset.

Summary

In this chapter we discovered the importance of building empathy with others. We examined the three channels of communication – body language, voice and words, and some tips on using each of the three channels to increase empathetic conversation. We learned how to avoid using verbal 'fouls' which only serve to drive wedges between people and how to listen to what others are saying. We also learned how to recognize and communicate with people of different behavioural styles to minimize conflict and build stronger relationships.

7

Using assertiveness

Never argue; repeat your assertion.

(Robert Owen, 1771–1858, British industrialist)

In this chapter we will explore the differences between three behaviours – aggressive, passive and assertive – and we will link them back to Chapter 4 on the fight and flight mechanism.

Our behavioural style influences our communication styles. If we tend to be fairly aggressive, we will probably dispense with niceties in our speech and our bluntness will often cause others to react adversely. If we are passive, we may drive people to distraction because we couch our words with so much padding that we sometimes never actually say what we mean.

This chapter will show how we can express ourselves in an appropriate manner – cleanly and clearly.

What is assertiveness?

Is assertiveness just another fad? When we talk about assertiveness training, some people think of it as some form of training, generally for women, on how to stand up for themselves. It is often thought of as a fad encouraged by feminists. Nothing could be further from the truth.

Assertiveness training is part of behavioural therapy and has been used for many years to help those who 'habitually fail to stand up for their rights' or 'who typically overreact with rage to real or imagined slights from others' (Kroger, 1963, p. 171). There are at least three possible behaviours we can exhibit in our interaction with others: aggressive, passive and assertive.

Assertive people are less likely to overreact in the event of conflict. They thus hold the reins of power and control. They are also respected and generally seen to be confident and authoritative. They are less likely to be picked upon, bullied or harassed.

Being assertive is being viewed as honest, open and forthright. People generally know where they stand with you.

The three behaviours are often regarded as a continuum or as degrees of behaviour ranging from two extremes – aggressive at one end and passive at the other, with assertiveness somewhere in the middle. Assertiveness training is often understood to tone down aggression or build up submissiveness. The middle ground is some sort of ideal.

Earlier, we discussed behaviours in conflict and related them to the general alarm response of fight and flight. But rather than thinking of the three behaviours as a continuum, we can regard them as separate behaviours. Two are the result of reaction or listening to ourselves and one is the result of a considered response or listening to others. Since we have a choice, we can choose to respond rather than to react. Fight and flight behaviour is a *reaction*; flow behaviour is a *response*.

What if I can't help my reactions? It can be useful to think of our brains in terms of a computer and our programmed learning and reactions as part of the data that we have input.

The difference between a computer, no matter how sophisticated, and our brains is that we can continue to input data and not worry about our brain cells filling up or an error message flashing 'Insufficient memory – shut down one of your current thoughts' across our eyes.

With a computer we know that correct input provides correct output, or in technobabble: garbage in, garbage out. And yet, we allow ourselves to react in counter-productive ways, and excuse our behaviour by saying that we could not help ourselves, as if our behaviour had nothing at all to do with us!

Like a computer, we also have a default mechanism. We can choose to override the default by choosing a different setting or to reprogramme the default mechanism. We can choose to do exactly the same with our thoughts and behavioural responses. Yet we constantly ignore this ability, preferring instead to justify erroneous behaviour retrospectively:

- 'I couldn't help it – there's something about John's manner that just makes me lose my cool.'
- 'I never seem to get those statistics right. I was never any good at numbers.'
- 'I may step on a few toes but I'm not paid to mollycoddle the staff and I always get the results.'

Do any of these sentiments sound familiar? And do they not sound ridiculous when you see them written down in black and white? If we can recognize them, then we can begin to do something about them.

Most of us have a good idea of our own behavioural patterns and realize where we need to make adjustments. This is why when completing psychometric tests, the answers often reflect how we know we should behave in a given situation rather than what we actually do.

Most people instantly recognize aggressive behaviour. However, it is interesting to note how many people confuse assertiveness with aggressive behaviour. While not wishing to fall into the trap of stereotyping people, it may be useful to build a picture of the three behavioural types referring back to the general alarm response of fight and flight (see Figure 7.1).

As we can see, whether we display aggressive or passive behaviour will depend on our *perception* of the event and our physiological reactions at the time. It is also context related.

What is aggressive behaviour?

Alternative words for aggressiveness are forceful, belligerent, pugnacious and contentious. Less complimentary words are vicious, warring, nasty and hostile.

Aggressive behaviour is associated with an increase in the hormone *noradrenaline*. Aggressive people want to win at any cost. They believe they have more rights than others and their needs are much more important. Consequently, they will speak more loudly, interrupt, bully, and use patronizing or sarcastic language. The intention behind their behaviour is 'I win, you lose'.

Their body language is often patronizing or intimidating, such as excessive staring or leaning over people. They will frequently invade your 'personal space' by moving closer to you, making you uncomfortable and forcing you to move back.

They will often gesticulate, prod and point. They will also offer

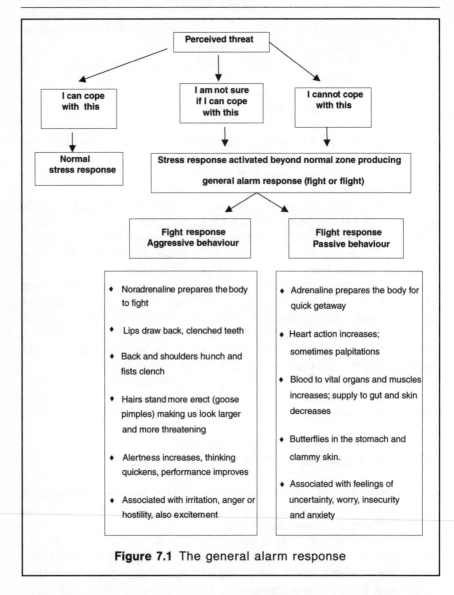

Figure 7.1 The general alarm response

a full frontal position that can be very threatening. Moving close to your face is another intimidating gesture.

Aggressive people will try to appear larger than they are. They will do everything possible to exaggerate this by puffing out their chests, putting their hands on their hips with elbows sticking out or pulling themselves to their full height, sometimes unconsciously standing up and down on their toes as they talk to you.

Dealing with aggressive behaviour

- Use your assertiveness skills.
- Acknowledge their emotions.
- Use active listening skills.
- Pace and lead them.
- Help them stay calm.
- Do not take it personally.
- Use neutral posture, tone of voice and facial expression.
- Maintain eye contact but do not try to outstare them.

What is passive behaviour?

Alternative words for passive are compliant, submissive, acquiescent and meek. Less complimentary words are servile, fawning, subservient and ingratiating.

Passive people are mainly influenced by the hormone *adrenaline*. Their prime concern is to avoid conflict, and they will not stand up for themselves if a confrontation is inevitable. Because of their extreme sensitivity, passive people will frequently see conflict where others do not.

Passive people tend to put others' needs before their own. They operate based on an 'I lose/You win' philosophy. They are often unaware of their own rights and will ignore them if they are. They lack confidence and self-esteem. They may believe their opinions are less valuable and are quick to agree with others. They tend to smile nervously and have great difficulty saying 'No'. Passive people can be extremely frustrating, often trying to wriggle out of making decisions or doing something on time.

Adrenaline increases their respiration rate making them draw breath before the end of a sentence. Their clammy hands may cause them to rub their hands together, giving the appearance of being even more nervous. They may also start shaking in a confrontation as the adrenaline prepares them for flight while they are immobile.

They speak in a lower and softer tone, and are often left out of conversations. In contrast to aggressive people, passive people try to look smaller than they are by bunching themselves up, wrapping their arms around themselves defensively. They look down trying to avoid eye contact. We observe this in many small animals that curl up when there is danger and they are unable to flee in time.

How to deal with passive behaviour

- Empathize.
- Be patient.
- Offer support.
- Use coaching skills to draw them out.
- Allow silences in your conversation.
- Ask open questions.
- Watch for non-verbal responses.
- Be firm and persistent.

Example, when introducing a new procedure that is likely to be unpopular:

- *Aggressive*: 'At our last management meeting we decided to make some long overdue changes. From now on, your expense claim forms must be submitted no later than the fifth of the following month. There will be no exceptions to this whatsoever. No claim form, no expenses paid. End of matter.'
- *Passive*: 'As you know, we have just had a management meeting and I'm afraid it's been decided to make some changes to the expense claims procedure. I'm afraid that it's not going to be popular, but ... er ... there is nothing we can do about it really. I hope you won't mind too much, but some of the accounts staff have been whingeing about late claim forms and, well, it's been decided not to accept any claim forms after the fifth of the following month.'
- *Assertive*: 'I'm calling this meeting to update you on the situation with late expense claim forms. This has caused the accounts department considerable problems and the management board has decided to tighten up procedure. We will not accept any claim form submitted after the fifth of the month. If any of you foresee an inability to meet this deadline, please let me know by the end of the month in question at the very latest and I'll do my best to help.

People rarely behave in one way all of the time; nor is it easy to separate behaviours into clearly defined categories. What is important is to become aware of the circumstances that lead you to one behaviour or another. For example, you may be very assertive with work colleagues yet be passive with your boss. Outside the workplace, you may display aggressive behaviour towards another. What factors are involved in how we choose our behaviour?

A useful model to examine our behaviour is adapted from Robert Dilts's (1990) neurological levels. This model allows you to organize your thinking in a logical sequential manner to help ascertain at which level the behavioural problem resides.

Exercise

Think of a particular incident when you wanted to stand up for yourself but did not, or of a situation in which you reacted in an inappropriately aggressive manner. It may help you to write down the different levels (see Figure 7.2) on squares of paper and lay them out on a table/desk or floor. Some people write them on large sheets of paper and stand on each level in turn to aid concentration. Do whichever suits you best.

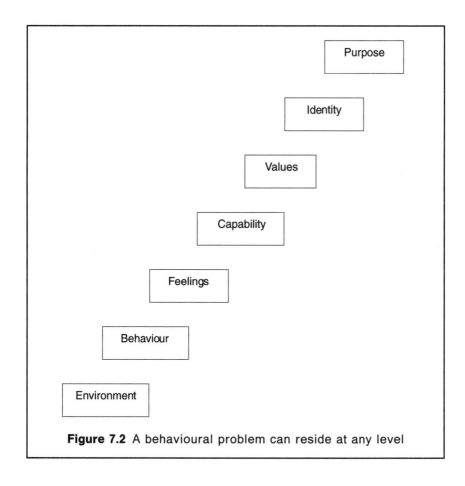

Figure 7.2 A behavioural problem can reside at any level

1. Level one is Environment (*the where and when*). In your mind's eye, go back to the exact location and time when the incident occurred. Take note of any particular circumstances that could have influenced your behaviour. For example, did the incident occur on your own territory or someone else's? How many people were involved? Were there any distractions? What time of the day was it? What type of a mood were you in? Were you sitting or standing? What were you seeing, hearing and feeling? Write down as many details as you can. Even those that you may think are unimportant could be a trigger or indicator that hold the clue to your behaviour.

2. Level two is Behaviour (*the what*). Turn to the actual behaviour, try to build a rich picture of the incident. What happened? What actual words were exchanged? What behaviours did you exhibit and how? What body language were you/others using? What thoughts were behind your behaviour, for example, 'I'm going to teach that person a lesson!' or 'Why is this person picking on me?'

3. Level three is Feelings (*the what else?*). Our feelings and emotions govern our behavioural patterns. If we feel happy, we respond differently than we do if we feel annoyed. If we feel fearful, we will react in one way and if we feel we have the upper hand, we may react in another. Can you remember how you were feeling at the time? If so, were you consciously aware of those feelings at the time? And if you had been would this have made a difference to the way you behaved?

4. Level four is Capability (*the how*). Having explored the first three levels, examine whether you know how to behave in any other manner. For example, if you exhibited passive behaviour, do you actually know how to stand up for yourself and act assertively? Are you familiar with any of the skills and techniques assertive people use? If you were behaving aggressively, do you know how to take control of your emotions? Do you know how to communicate the same message in a different manner? Learning to be assertive involves learning new skills and practising them till they become second nature.

5. Level five is Values (*the why*). How we behave is dictated by what we think and feel which, in turn, is influenced by our values and beliefs. No matter how capable we actually are, if we do not believe in ourselves then we are unlikely to even try. If you behaved inappropriately despite knowing what to do, then the answer is likely to reside at a higher level. What values and beliefs surrounded the issue in question? Do you

believe that your own needs and concerns are less important than those of the other person? Did you feel so strongly about the issue that you reacted aggressively? Or do you feel that in a case of conflict it is best to withdraw from the arena? This level, i.e. values and beliefs, is of great importance to your behaviour. By seeking any negative or self-limiting beliefs, you will find it much easier to behave in a more assertive manner.

6. Level six is Identity (*the who*). You are the sum of your behaviours, capabilities, values and beliefs. Some people have a very strong sense of who they are while others are still striving to find themselves. Having a strong sense of identity will enable you to act in a measured and appropriate manner. Returning to the incident under examination, concentrate on your own identity throughout the incident. Were you aware of a strong sense of identity? Was it threatened in any way? How did the issue affect you as a person? Was your behaviour in keeping with your basic sense of self, your very core or did it feel in some way alien to your identity? Without a strong sense of identity, you may be taken advantage of by others and are more likely to react in an unhelpful manner.

7. Level seven is Purpose (*who else*). At this level, the highest level, we are considering how we are connected to the universe and to others outside ourselves. Why are we here and what is our purpose? Religious beliefs do not necessarily influence this thinking, although this may be the case with some people. It has to do with a feeling of interconnection. It can be very powerful to realize that there is more to the world than just us and our own needs. In terms of the event under examination, you may wish to reflect if anything or anyone else was involved in your behaviour. Who else might care about this? Who else might be affected or involved? What else might be at stake?

Consider all the thoughts that come into your mind. Many of them will appear unbidden and may seem to bear no relevance to the incident upon which you have been reflecting. No matter, let the thoughts flow over, around and into you and allow yourself to feel whatever you are feeling.

When you are ready, start reviewing the incident from the top down. Reconsider each level from your newer, higher, perspective, moving back down the levels to environment. By now you should have a stronger sense of the reason behind your behaviour. By similarly reflecting on other examples, you may find a pattern emerging. It may be that you do not have the skills or tools to deal with your own reactions or that you hold particular values and beliefs that consistently prevent you from using them appropriately.

Exercise

It can be useful to create a hierarchy of situations and people with whom you find difficulty in asserting yourself. Here are some examples:

People: where applicable, name actual people. Otherwise, list categories or groups of people, e.g.

- my boss
- my colleagues
- people in authority
- people who report to me
- superior sales people
- my father/ mother
- my accountant/general practitioner
- Paul/Jane/Carol.

Situations:

- saying 'No' at work
- refusing invitations to events I do not wish to attend
- being firm with my friends' misbehaving children
- disciplining subordinates at work
- standing up for myself with the boss

Once you become aware of the people and the situations with which you have particular difficulty, and the level at which this difficulty occurs, you will find it much easier to act appropriately.

If you do not feel confident, act as if you are. Or, if you cannot make it, fake it. You would be surprised how many seemingly confident people employ this technique. If we pretend for long enough, we become what we pretend to be. We can fool our brains into thinking we are assertive by adopting assertive postures and mannerisms. Time spent in cultivating an assertive voice and using assertive body language is well worth while.

Exercise

One approach that produces quite dramatic results is modelling. Think of one person whom you respect and admire. The chances are that this person has personal power, charisma and is confident and assertive in their behaviour. If you can find a photograph of this person to refer to while doing the exercise, that is ideal. If not, you will have to rely on the powers of your imagination.

Place the photograph, or recall a mental image, of the person in question. Now, on a sheet of blank paper write down the qualities that you most admire in him or her. Consider some of the following aspects:

- Posture: upright with straight shoulders; relaxed, alert manner.
- Facial expression: often open and pleasant without being obsequious or threatening.
- Body language: open gestures and confident mannerisms; appropriate distance observed.
- Voice: calm; low to medium pitch; pace and volume gauged to suit listener; appropriate inflections.

Imagine how your chosen role model would deal with a tricky situation. Now, try to emulate this behaviour. Next time you feel you are not behaving as you would wish, ask yourself 'how would (chosen person) deal with this?' As with any technique, it pays to practise it in a safe environment a few times before trying it out in a tricky real-life situation.

Why is it sometimes difficult to say something to one person and yet not to another?

- The time or place may not be right.
- You may be afraid of the other person's reaction.
- You may not want to offend that person or hurt their feelings.
- You may not know how to word your feelings appropriately.
- You may lack confidence in your own position.
- You may be denying your rights or feelings.

Sometimes when we are in conflict with another person, it is as if we are on either side of a solid brick wall. We shout out to each other across the wall, each firmly stuck on our own side, smug in the belief that we are right and they are wrong. And yet, if we stepped sideways or used a ladder to climb up and look over the wall, we would find that the wall was not as high or as wide as we had imagined. If only we could find a foolproof way to communicate across brick walls!

Two techniques which assertive people use regularly are 'I' statements and 'broken record'. Both are invaluable to add to your assertiveness repertoire.

An 'I' statement is where you express your feelings about a situation without using a phrase beginning with 'You'. It is useful to imagine the word 'you' as an accusing finger being jabbed into another person. You can make 'I' statements to:

- clarify your own feelings to yourself about an issue which is bothering you
- communicate clearly and calmly your perception of and feelings about a problem without attacking, blaming or hurting the other person
- open a discussion without eliciting defensiveness from the other person.

To start getting used to 'I' statements, formulate one to yourself whenever someone or something causes you concern. We tend to do this anyway, but usually negatively. For example, you are presenting a proposal at a meeting and a dismissive colleague constantly interrupts you. If you bite your tongue and carry on, you are likely to leave the meeting with the whole scene replaying in your mind. 'Smug so and so, how dare he be so patronizing' or 'that cow – trying to score points off me' and so on. You are likely to go over and over the matter, unable to let go.

This is the point at which you can formulate an 'I' statement to yourself. 'When I am interrupted before I can present my ideas fully, I feel undermined and disrespected. I also feel angry that none of the others at the meeting told him or her to keep quiet. What I would like is that I could finish my presentation completely and then field questions. I would also like the questions to be asked in a neutral and non-patronizing manner.'

By acknowledging your feelings and what you would like to happen instead, you have empowered yourself. You have regained some control over the situation. Expressing your feelings in this manner produces a cathartic effect. There, you have said it. Now what are you going to do about it?

Table 7.1 Rules for making 'I' statements

1. *The issue or action in question*	Describe it objectively and assertively	Start with 'When'; use 'I'; avoid using 'You'	*When I* am not able to finish what I am saying . . .; *When I* am not invited to strategy meetings . . .
2. *How it makes me feel*	Do not blame the other person; use appropriate tone and body language	I feel like . . . or I feel . . .	*I feel like* taking my ideas elsewhere; *I feel* undervalued/ disrespected
3. *What I would like to happen instead*	Do not make unreasonable demands; use appropriate assertiveness	And what I would like is to/that I . . .	*is to* complete what I want to say . . .; *that I* be more involved in decision-making processes

You can now choose whether to bring the subject up with your colleague or not. You may find that next time it happens, you will feel more confidence in expressing how you are feeling and what you would like instead.

Use your 'I' statements regularly to yourself until they feel comfortable. You may be surprised to hear yourself using one without even thinking about it.

An 'I' statement comprises three elements. Each element has its own set of rules. Table 7.1 shows the formula.

Depending on the response of the other person, choose an appropriate next action. It may be to make another 'I' statement, use active listening skills, or discuss the issue in more detail or some other purpose.

Exercise

Consider an issue that is causing you concern and which you wish to raise with another person. In your workbook, note down what you would like to say. Now, using the above formula, convert it to an 'I' statement.

The formula gets easier with practice. Soon, you will find that you can make the statement simply by using the middle section: 'I feel confused', 'I feel frustrated with the delay', 'I'm feeling out of my depth'.

The philosophy behind an 'I' statement is ownership of your feelings. Notice that the phrase is always 'I feel' never 'You make me feel'. Eleanor Roosevelt is believed to have said 'Nobody can make you feel inferior without your permission'. I take this one step further and say 'Nobody can make you feel *anything* without your permission'.

Taking ownership of your statements also extends to simple phrases such as 'I didn't express myself clearly enough' rather than 'You don't understand what I'm saying'. There is a great sense of power and liberation in taking control of your own destiny and expressing yourself in this manner.

How do you say 'No' in the face of repeated requests and, occasionally, emotional blackmail? How else can you express your needs calmly, persistently and assertively – particularly in the face of anger or unreasonableness?

One technique to use is the broken record. Remember the old vinyl records? If they were scratched, the needle would often stick at a point where the same bit of the song or melody would repeat itself over and over again.

You can do the same thing if you keep repeating, more or less, the same statement over and over again in a calm and controlled voice. In the face of anger, it is very easy to be provoked into reacting irrationally, answering irrelevant points or being goaded into defence. By using the broken record you can simply keep on track and defer making rash statements until you have had more time think about the issue.

Stick to the same story and do not allow yourself to be sidetracked. During a recent activity I was facilitating, two trainees were role-playing a holidaymaker wanting to borrow money from a holiday representative. The holiday company's policy prohibited her from lending company money. The following exchange occurred:

> *Holidaymaker*: I wouldn't ask if I weren't desperate. I can pay it back to you by early next week.
> *Rep*: I'm sorry. It is against our company policy to lend money.
> *Holidaymaker*: I've arranged for money to be transferred to the local bank. I am willing to sign any forms required.
> *Rep*: I do understand your situation. However, it is against our company policy.
> *Holidaymaker*: This is the worst customer service I have ever come across. In all my years of going abroad, I

have never had to ask for a loan before and I wouldn't do it if I had any other alternative. Let me speak to your manager.

Rep: I'm sorry you are in this situation but we are strictly forbidden to lend company money ... other than in emergencies.

Holidaymaker (grasping this new opening to try another tack): But this *is* an emergency.

The rules are clear. Do not deviate from the same message. You may add an occasional padding or change a minor word but stick to the same overall message.

Do you know your rights?

These days, it seems everyone knows his or her rights. And if they do not, well, there is bound to be a civil liberties group that will put them wise. This is often taken to extremes as one group's rights infringes another's. For example, the right to smoke in public versus the right not to have to inhale other people's smoke, or the right to listen to a personal stereo system on public transport versus the right not to have to listen to the maddening leaks from other people's headphones. We are all entitled by the virtue of our very existence to have and express our own feelings, wants and needs.

Aggressive people will attempt to claim all their rights with no consideration for the rights of others. In other words, rights without responsibilities. Passive people, on the other hand, will deny their own rights, while making sure everyone else's wants, whether right or wrong, are considered first. An assertive person will claim their rights, and extend the same privilege to others.

Rights must be balanced by responsibilities. You may have a right to freedom but this must be tempered by your responsibility to others and respect for their rights to freedom too.

Non-assertive or passive people often have difficulty in accepting their own rights although they are quick to accept these rights for others. It is as though they give their rights away, and with it their personal power. They will be quick to defend other people – 'I'm sure she didn't mean it', 'Don't worry, he is just having a bad day', 'He was doing his best', 'With her background, you can understand why she did that' – and yet be very hard on themselves – 'I should never have said that', 'When will

I ever learn', 'I make one mistake after another', 'I should have known better'.

Exercise

Here is a list of common assertive rights. Read through the list and consider your responses to each. Finally, add a few of your own.

I have the right to:

- be treated with respect and consideration
- hold my own views and have them heard
- remain silent
- have my feelings taken seriously
- make my own decisions and cope with the consequences
- make my own choices
- make mistakes
- change my mind
- choose when and if to assert myself
- refuse without feeling guilty
- get what I pay for
- ask for what I want
- ask for information about myself
- be given an explanation
- privacy.

Others:

> All rights involve responsibilities. I believe in extending to others any right I claim as my own.

Assertiveness – a safety warning

If you have had difficulty asserting yourself in the past, you may find that becoming assertive initially creates more problems than it solves. Colleagues may grumble about 'how the worm has turned' and tell you that you were a 'more pleasant' person before you started this assertiveness mumbo jumbo. Well, of course! A passive person can often be overlooked or counted on to join in with the majority decision. They can be persuaded to do overtime, cover extended lunch hours, make an extra cup of coffee, go to the post office or run an errand for somebody else in their own lunch hours.

Being assertive does not prevent you from doing any of these things if you really want to. The payback is that you will not feel pressured into doing something you did not want to do and end up feeling resentful and angry.

Remember, too, that non-assertive or passive people rarely are promoted. They may be regarded as 'nice' but they will not be considered 'management material'.

Aggressive people fare no better. Although it often seems unfair that aggressive behaviour, often referred to as Rottweiler management, is sometimes rewarded with higher positions and more money and status, in the long term such behaviour is untenable. Not only is this type of management culture going out of fashion, but human resource and employment legislation is also speeding its demise.

Significantly, people who have been on assertiveness courses, often choose assertiveness as a behavioural model without any persuasion. It increases confidence, improves relationships and restores self-respect. This enables them to handle conflict more effectively. A large return on a relatively small investment!

Summary

In this chapter we considered the difference between reaction and response. Behaving aggressively or passively are often reactions, while behaving assertively is a response that requires more skills and confidence.

The intention behind our communication is paramount. The underlying message may be aggressive or passive even if we couch it in assertive terms. No assertiveness techniques will work if they are used with contradicting body language.

By becoming assertive, we improve our relationships, maximize the chances of being understood, and thus increase our ability to resolve conflicts.

8

Handling power constructively

> Mastering others is strength, mastering yourself is true power.
>
> (Lao-Tzu, 604–531 BC, Chinese philosopher)

Some people refer to conflict as power struggles. No doubt, power is a main part of any conflict. This chapter will explore our attitudes to power, power bases and how we use and abuse them. We will also differentiate between having power over people and having power with people. We will also consider self-empowerment and its value in increasing our self-confidence.

Our concept of power

Most of us will have some concept of what we actually mean by the word 'power'. In word association activities, here are some of the most commonly mentioned: influence, force, money, authority, abuse, politics, position, armed force, reward, punishment, energy, control, coercion, manipulation, victim, aggression.

Some people view power as positive, others as negative. Some have an emotional response to it and some look at the possible consequences.

Exercise

On a piece of paper write down the names of colleagues with whom you have the most contact. A recommended maximum

101

manageable number would be 15. The list may include suppliers, rivals and clients. Now give them a power rating, in whichever way you rate power, on a scale of 1 to 10, with 1 being least powerful and 10 being most powerful.

Now, rewrite the names, including your own, in list form with those whom you consider to be the most powerful at the top and the least powerful at the bottom. You now have your immediate hierarchy of power. Take some time to reconsider this list. You may find that you wish to amend, delete, add or simply move names around. Where have you positioned yourself? When you are completely satisfied, consider the following:

- What does power mean to you?
- Who has power over you?
- Over whom do you have power?
- With whom do you feel powerful?
- With whom do you feel powerless?
- How do you give away your power?

Many of us have never stopped to consider our relationship with power or even that we attribute power to some people and not to others. And yet, the name at the top of your list may come in the middle or even near the bottom of someone else's hierarchy. The same applies to the name at the very bottom of your list. They too exert some power over others.

Power bases

It is more than likely that you will have placed yourself in a middle position in your hierarchy of power. Now imagine that each of these two groups were to ask you to carry out a task which you did not particularly wish to do. Of the two groups, whose request would you find it more difficult to say 'No' to? You may even find it difficult to imagine someone very low down the power hierarchy ever having the temerity to ask you to carry out any task at all!

You should have been able to name one or more persons to whom you would find it difficult to refuse a request. What power do these people have over you? What makes you defer to them? You have now ascertained their power bases.

A number of power bases have been found, for example, French and Raven's (1958) study. Here are some generally accepted categories. You may have identified some of your own which do not quite fit into any of these. If so, try to give them a name and see if you attribute these categories to others whom you perceive to have power over you.

1. *Reward or punishment power.* If someone can motivate you by recognition and praise, or punish you by imposing penalties, then this is a form of power. Appraisals are a form of power. Physical or verbal abuse and emotional blackmail also come under this category. Many of us will recall our distress at a playground friend's 'If you don't give me your Teddy bear, I won't be your friend again'. Even at an early age some of us abuse power.

2. *Positional power.* The lines of power may be blurred in some types of organization but we always know instinctively who has power and why: your boss, or others to whom you report. Other positional powers could come from authority, for example the Inland Revenue, police or social services. Positional power may also refer to someone working for someone in authority, for example, a secretary who controls access to his or her boss. Someone in an intimate relationship with a powerful person also has some measure of power, the 'power behind the throne'.

3. *Expertise/knowledge power.* A person can have power over you because you respect their superior or specific knowledge and expertise. An information technology (IT) manager may have expert power over a board of directors if they are dependent on him or her. Another form of knowledge power is where someone has received some inside or advance knowledge which can be used as a weapon or bargaining tool over somebody.

4. *Personal power/charisma.* Some people are born with it and others have to work very hard to cultivate just a little. Charismatic people have no difficulty persuading others to their point of view or to do things for them. Such people are respected simply for whom they are. When allied to another power base, as well, it becomes an unbeatable combination. Sir John Harvey-Jones, a British management guru is quoted by Crainer (1997, p. 249) as saying 'Positions of power are by definition, ephemeral, while one's personal characteristics remain with one until death'.

5. *Relationship power.* When you defer to somebody because they are important to you, you would not want to upset them or you want to keep their goodwill, this is relationship power.

You may also defer to somebody on occasion because you may want something from them at a later date: 'I'm calling in the favour. You owe me one.'

6. *Collective power*. A typical example of collective power would be trade unions. A person on their own may not have much power but allied to others with similar values, beliefs and goals they become a power to be reckoned with. Collective power misused may result in coercion.

7. *Cooperative power*. People from the different sides of a fence, so to speak, who work together in order to achieve their goals and outcomes are demonstrating cooperative power. It differs from collective power in that the 'opposing' factors gain the power from working together to resolve matters rather than against each other. Peter Drucker, a management thinker, said 'Adversarial power relationships work only if you never have to see or work with the bastards again' (quoted in Crainer, 1997, p. 248).

8. *Legislative power*. Legislative power is an interesting power base to consider. New legislation, particularly from the European Union, has endowed some people with powers that were non-existent some years ago. Consider the new equality laws and disability Acts. While overall beneficial, these laws have on occasion allowed people to hide behind them while acting in an inappropriate manner. A person may be guilty of gross misconduct but will appeal against dismissal by claiming racial or sexual harassment.

9. *Physical power*. This power is rarely recognized in organizational behaviour. However, it is a power that we often acknowledge at an unconscious level. 'You wouldn't want to interfere with him!' Some people will cultivate their physical power by weight training when they realize that they are lacking in any other power base. Physical power comes into its own in an angry confrontation between two people of unequal stature or strength. If there is a conflict in your office and you cannot ascertain any recognized power base, it may be useful to examine the physical aspects of the parties involved.

The 'power thing' is not constant. It is often context dependent and the power can shift from one side to another during the course of a conflict.

James, the accounts manager is in conflict with Charles, the marketing director. Charles initially holds the balance of power as he is in a higher position in the hierarchy than James (positional power). Subsequently, James discovers something that could put Charles's position in jeopardy. The balance of power moves to James (knowledge power). Much as in a game of chess, each move is carefully calculated and the one with the current power balance can checkmate.

Exercise

Consider a conflict with which you are either currently involved or have been involved with in the past. On a piece of paper write the names of the protagonists. Now, list the initial hierarchy of power and their power bases. Analyse the stages of the conflict and the power shifts that occurred.

- Did the power bases and hierarchies remain constant?
- Were you aware of these power bases at the time?
- Was there any misuse of power by any of the parties?
- If the conflict has been resolved, how did this come about?
- Did you notice a shift in the power bases and hierarchies towards the end?

A frequent source of conflict in the workplace these days is management of change. More than ever, managers have to introduce and implement changes, some of which create massive resistance. If these are not properly handled, there is a risk that the organization will polarize into those for the change and those against it. Thereafter, some members of staff will simply oppose or sabotage any and every suggestion, decision or policy proposed.

As a manager, you have the power of authority. Resistant staff have collective power. Suppose you need to introduce a new procedure that you know will be unpopular. How would you go about implementing this with a resistant workforce?

You will probably be faced with three choices: you can coerce, manipulate or influence. It is the intention behind the communication that matters.

Coercion is an overtly aggressive approach: 'I win/you lose', 'Do it or else...'. Manipulation is covert aggression. It is still 'I win/you lose'. Manipulation by praise is common: 'You're so good at this, you do it.'

Influencing is an assertive and respectful approach. It is a 'win/win' approach. Persuading people is quite different from

Table 8.1 Main differences between manipulation/coercion and influencing

Manipulation and coercion	Influencing
Against	*For*
Win/lose approach	Win/win approach
Destroys staff motivation and commitment	Gains staff motivation and commitment
Establishes adversarial relationships	Everyone's needs are considered
Promotes cynicism and mistrust	Staff feel persuaded and respected
Signifies poor leadership	Allows time for discussion
Does not allow staff input	Helps build better relationships
Information may be biased	Encourages creativity
Decisions rushed through	Encourages better quality decisions
For	*Against*
Possibly effective in short term	Could be time-consuming
May be suitable where urgency/secrecy is paramount	

manipulating them. One is above board and the other uses guile and deception. Manipulation and coercion use force and trickery to achieve the desired solution. Influencing uses integrity and rationality.

What are some of the main differences between each of the two approaches at work? The answers are in Table 8.1.

Influencing using reason, rationale and discussion usually beats coercion and manipulation.

One useful model for influencing others is the five-step PEPSI approach. The reason some people fail to influence is they only use the first and third steps – the two Ps, commonly known as whingeing!

1. *Position.* State the current position objectively: 'John, I understand you've refused my request to attend next week's customer relations training.'
2. *Empathize.* Be positive. Understand their point of view: 'I do understand that being away for the day will cause a delay in processing the outstanding enquiries, and I am just as keen as you are to clear the backlog.'
3. *Problem.* State what problem the occurrence has caused and who is affected: 'However, this course covers important new legislation, which will affect our operations. If we don't comply we are likely to find ourselves in serious trouble.'
4. *Solutions.* Present alternative possible solutions: 'There are three possibilities we can consider: you could delegate

someone else to attend and run an induction course for us; we could arrange to have the course run in-house for us during low season; or you could reconsider and allow me to go.'

5. *Influence.* Use charisma and reason to persuade others to your solution: 'Running the course in-house will be more expensive and waiting till low season will be too late. Finding someone else who is free next week at short notice may be difficult. I would really appreciate it if you reconsidered my request. What I will do in return is to work an extra day at the weekend, and take an extra day off in lieu when we are quieter.

Power relationships

Often we assume roles in relationships. These roles may suit us and may not cause us any difficulties. On the other hand, if there is an abuse of power by either side, then the relationship has to be re-examined.

Our power bases easily change according to context. For example, in a relationship where the husband is a bully, the terrified wife could be very surprised to see that her husband is afraid of his boss.

Transactional analysis (TA) (Berne, 1964; Harris, 1973) is a system of psychotherapy that focuses on the interactional aspect of communication. Transactional analysis postulates three distinct states from which a person may be operating at any one time. These are:

- Parent: nurturing or controlling. This is our ethical state.
- Child: natural or adapted. This is our feeling state.
- Adult. This is our thinking state.

For example, someone may speak to you in a way that reminds you of how your parents spoke to you in the past, triggering off a child state. Hardly the most appropriate response in an adult and certainly not in a working environment.

Harris's work centred on these three states and the basic worth of human beings and how they perceived other people's worth. He called this 'OK-ness' and defined four positions which we will use in considering power relationships. Some British managers struggle with the concept of being 'OK', finding it too American for their tastes. I translate the concept into one of self-worth or self-esteem. 'OK-ness' is how highly we value ourselves, and

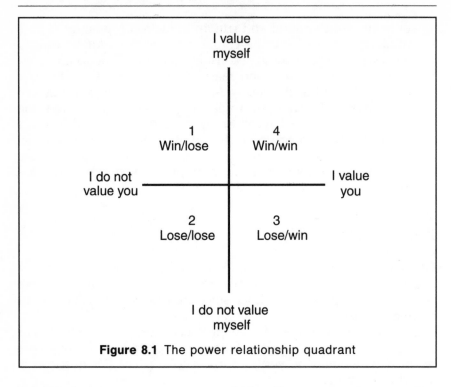

Figure 8.1 The power relationship quadrant

echoes the cosmetics company L'Oreal's concept 'because I'm worth it'.

Figure 8.1 models the four quadrants of the power relationship concept. Each quadrant has its own common traits:

- Quadrant 1: aggressive, arrogant, domineering; patronizing, rigid.
- Quadrant 2: hostile, low energy, apathetic, lacking initiative.
- Quadrant 3: compliant, inadequate, passive, servile, pleasers.
- Quadrant 4: assertive, confident, responsive, high self-esteem.

Miscommunications arise if people speak to each other from different ego states and TA is commonly used in communication and people management skills, for example:

> *Jane* (asking in adult state): 'Have you seen that Bothwell file? I had it on my desk yesterday but I can't find it anywhere.'
> *Mary* (answering in parent state): 'How many times have I told you to keep your desk clear? This wouldn't happen if you were more organized.'

The above response could provoke Jane into responding in a child-like manner, for example: 'It's my desk and I'll keep it as messy as I please.' Or she could choose to stay in adult state: 'Mary, when I'm spoken to like that, I feel irritated. I thought you may have borrowed the file but since you haven't seen it, I'll ask Jerry if he's got it.'

Being aware of our ego states is useful as misunderstanding often arises from this sort of cross-communication.

Bullying at work is being increasingly identified as one of the main sources of stress and conflict. However, a bully thrives on the victim's passive behaviour. One cannot exist without the other. What type of behaviour does each commonly exhibit? See Table 8.2 for the answers.

Some of the behaviours in Table 8.2 are immediately recognizable, others are so well hidden that we may never realize that we have been unknowing victims.

One person I spoke to told me that it was only after she learnt about power issues that she became aware of her victim-type behaviour. 'I realized' she said 'that it was almost as if I had been walking around in a T-shirt emblazoned with the slogan "Victim – available for next persecutor". I was constantly bemoaning my fate – I was so unlucky I had one dreadful boss after another. Little did I realize that it was my own behaviour that brought out the worst in them.'

Some of us will know of, or have heard about, people who go from one abusive relationship to another or – on a more prosaic level – people who constantly fall in love with those who betray

Table 8.2 Bullying and victim behaviours

Bullying behaviour	Victim's behaviour
Punish	Helpless
Criticize	Poor me
Pick on	Martyr
Harass	Blame everyone around them
Bulldoze	Blaming circumstances and upbringing
Coerce	Inadequate
Embarrass	Defeated
Humiliate	Bitter
Shout at	Constantly complaining
Abuse	Passive
Assault	Apathetic
Subdue	Stuck
Blackmail – emotionally or otherwise	Anxious or depressed

Table 8.3 How bullies and victims can change their behaviour

Bullies could	Victims could
Empathize	Stand up for themselves
Listen	Listen
Communicate assertively	Take responsibility
Consult with others	Learn to be assertive
Share their expertise	Look at situations objectively
Reconnect with their conscience	Identify their needs
Share decision-making	Look towards the future rather than
Give constructive feedback	wallowing in the past
Help build people's self-confidence	Take action to bring about solutions
and morale	

their trust and break their hearts. You may even have heard yourself saying 'When will they ever learn!' Once you are aware of the problem, you are halfway towards solving it. After all, if you are acting in a way that has people chorusing 'victim!' and playing an imaginary violin in the air, it does not need an expert to tell you what to do.

Bullies by their very nature are often socially inadequate, less aware and immune to other people's feelings. That is why the emphasis is first placed on helping the 'victims' stand up for themselves. How can bullies and victims change their behaviour to help themselves? (See Table 8.3.)

In both new behaviours active listening and assertive communication form a link. In fact, these are core skills in changing behaviour and moving out of power game relationships.

The energies of these relationships are such that if a victim decides to take responsibility and stand up for themselves, the bully will no longer torment him or her – but may move on to another victim if they do not change their own behaviour.

The power balance

In any relationship between two or more people, there exists a delicate power balance. One party can have more power, equal power or less power.

We are not always consciously aware of this power balance but we are always aware of who is the more powerful at an unconscious level. Like animals, we are also fiercely territorial and people who encroach upon our personal space (territory) are seen as a threat.

Exercise

Try this experiment next time you are having a meal sitting opposite someone whom you do not know intimately – a business lunch is ideal. Run an imaginary line across the table to equally divide the table into your territory and theirs. Very subtly move the condiments into 'their' space and watch the reaction. In most cases, you will notice that they become uncomfortable and they will start to nudge them back into the middle of the table – where you drew the imaginary line. Some people may retaliate by pushing the salt and pepper onto 'your' half of the table. Most of the time, they will not be aware of what they are doing.

Dealing with powerful people

You may be surprised to find, having read this far, that dealing with powerful people no longer intimidates you. By removing the mystique from the concept of power, we find ourselves better able to deal with it.

I am reminded here of the story of the Zen master who drew a line on the sand and asked his pupil how he could make it shorter. The pupil could not think how. The Zen master then drew a longer line beside the first one. 'Now', he said, 'the line is shorter'. In exactly the same way, we need to plan a strategy to strengthen ourselves rather than weakening the opponent.

There are myriad reasons why you might come into conflict with someone. It could be as simple as a mutual dislike. If you have to work directly with that person then it is in your interest to lay the foundations for a more harmonious working relationship. Here are some strategies to help:

1. *Build up your own power by approaching them confidently and assertively*. Deal with your own emotions first. Do you feel nervous or anxious? These will spill over and get in the way of your discussion. Never fawn over powerful people. It may feed their vanity and sense of importance but they will never respect you for it. An open, confident, and assertive approach will serve your needs far better.
2. *Strengthen your own power bases*. What is your power base? How can you build on that? What further information or resources might you need? There could be rules, regulations or precedents there to help.

3. *Build empathy with the other person*. Use all your skills to build empathy with the other person.
4. *Look for a win/win*. What are your needs? What are the other person's needs? How can we reach a collaborative solution here? What issues are really important and which can we let go of?

If you need to persuade a more powerful person to your cause prepare your groundwork thoroughly and make sure you have contingency plans for each possible objection. Present your case clearly and unemotionally, backed up with facts and figures. Declare any vested interest before the other person finds out. Be prepared to be flexible and to consider other options or alternatives. This makes it easier for the other person to say 'Yes'. Enlist support, if necessary, but make sure it does not look like coercion.

How to deal with someone more powerful than you is common sense. If the person is reasonable, there should be no problem. If he or she is unreasonable then you will need to plan a careful strategy. There is not much to be gained by open confrontation. You may need to bide your time or sacrifice short-term benefits for long-term ones.

Increasing your personal power

One of the power bases we discussed was personal power or charisma. This sort of power is a result of your personality, not of any external source such as position or knowledge, although they may add the finishing touches.

Exercise

Think of someone whose charisma you admire. What personal qualities is this power built on?

I ask this question frequently in my workshops and the answers are always surprisingly similar: confidence, energy, humour, unruffled, self-aware, know where they are going, influential, calm, persuasive, well turned out, in control, responsive, intuitive, popular. Add your own:

Next I ask, 'How many of these traits do you recognize in yourself?' Most participants will list some of them but underestimate their own personal power. This occasionally arises from modesty but is often a genuine lack of awareness of their own positive qualities. If we are not aware of the full extent of our power or potential power, then we will act as though we are less powerful than we really are. By under-estimating our power, we are giving it away.

Another way we give away our power is to use disempowering language. I have a friend who always starts her telephone conversations with 'It's only me'. Here are some others you might recognize:

- 'I'm just a secretary.'
- 'Nobody listens to you/us/me around here.'
- 'I'm no good with computers.'
- 'It's only a suggestion and probably not a very good one...'

Another common turn of phrase used by disempowered people is 'you' when referring to themselves: 'You slog your guts out around here and nobody appreciates you.'

One way to regain control of our lives is to overcome the notion of 'shoulding', 'musting' and 'having to':

- 'I suppose I'll have to go to that meeting.'
- 'I should really do the filing.'
- 'I ought to go to the gym this evening.'

This is the tyranny of the 'should'. It indicates that you are not in charge. Some pressure from authority, past or present, is running the show. This sort of tape playing in your mind can cause enormous stress.

However, it is possible to change the above statements to 'I choose'. Instead of 'having to go to the meeting' you can say that you 'choose to go to the meeting'. You may argue that it is semantics but the power of language is such that by altering your phrases, you also alter your perception of the event and thus your response to it.

The way 'I must clear my desk before going on holiday' is phrased is likely to make you think 'Why should I? It's such a chore'. This soon leads to 'Its hardly worth going on holiday' and before long you are in a thoroughly foul mood. You have a choice of two actions: You can either submit to this dreadful chore or you can rebel and not clear your desk. If you clear your desk you will feel resentful and frustrated, and if you do not you will feel guilty. Such emotions will simmer below the surface and push you to getting your own back somehow. Normally, this is achieved through acting the martyr (victim) or taking it out on someone else (persecutor). This perpetuates the cycle.

If we phrased the above sentence as 'I choose to (or I'd like to) clear my desk before my holiday' we are putting an entirely different complexion on the matter. We then have less pressure and our choice is entirely our own. We clear our desk or we do not clear our desk. Having made the choice, we then accept the consequences. 'I have chosen not to clear my desk and if some emergency or unforeseen circumstance arises while I am away, I shall have to deal with it when I get back.' This enables you to take responsibility for your action, which leads you to a personal freedom from pressure. When you agree to take responsibility for your own actions – to discover what the consequences are and learn from them – you become less cautious, less afraid and more ready to learn from your experiences – a state of discovery.

Shoulding others

Not content with using shoulds and musts on ourselves, we are often guilty of using them on other people too: 'You shouldn't approach him in that manner'; 'You ought to stand up for yourself more.'

This demand behaviour results in exactly the same consequences as we saw before. The person we are 'shoulding' feels patronized and pressured. He or she will probably feel annoyed and may well tell you to mind your own business. Even if your intentions are good, there are better ways of approaching people.

Exercise

Think of a person that you have recently thought should or should not behave in a particular manner, i.e. 'He or she should exert more authority over his or her staff'. Consider Figure 8.2. Cover column 2 with a piece of paper and write down your replies to the questions in column 1. When you have finished, uncover column 2 and check whether your replies contained any of the behaviours described.

Now turn to Figure 8.3. Using the same example as you selected previously, cover column 2 with a piece of paper and answer the questions in column 1. When you have finished, uncover

COLUMN 1	COLUMN 2
What behaviour do you think the person should change?	Is there a desire to control? Or a misguided intention of helping
Why do you think the person behaves this way?	Are you criticizing or being judgemental?
How do you think the person should behave? How do you communicate that to them?	Are you demanding that they conform to your standards of behaviour? Are you being bossy or manipulative?
How might the person respond to your 'should'?	Are they angry, frustrated, uncooperative? Or are they acting like martyrs?
Depending on the person's response, what might you do next?	Would you reward or punish them in some way?

Figure 8.2 Demanding
Source: Reprinted with permission from Fiona Hollier, Kerrie Murray and Helena Cornelius (1993) *Conflict Resolution Trainers Manual: 12 Skills*, Conflict Resolution Network, Australia, H.5.8.

column 2 and see if your answers contained any of the behaviours mentioned.

Notice that we always have behavioural choices. We can choose to demand and persecute or we can choose to collaborate and support. We can choose to become victims or we can choose to empower ourselves. How we choose to behave affects how others behave. By discovering and using our power appropriately, we can influence with integrity. Margaret Thatcher sums up power beautifully: 'Being powerful is like being a lady. If you have to tell people you are, then you aren't' (quoted in Crainer, 1997, p. 250).

Summary

In this chapter we examined our own concept of power. We observed how people can use different power bases to achieve

COLUMN 1	COLUMN 2
What is the issue you want to work on? (Separate the person from the issue)	Notice that you are now cooperating with the other person.
What is the other person's perspective? What are their needs?	You are now using win/win tactics. There is no judgement or blame
What is the outcome you want or that is required? How can that be achieved or communicated?	You are now willing to enquire and listen. You are looking at the other person's perspective.
How might the other person respond to your desired outcome?	They have a free choice to agree or disagree. This encourages them to accept the consequences and take responsibility for their future actions.

Figure 8.3 Influencing
Source: Reprinted with permission from Fiona Hollier, Kerrie Murray and Helena Cornelius (1993) *Conflict Resolution Trainers Manual: 12 Skills*, Conflict Resolution Network, Australia, H.5.9.

their ends and learnt to recognize subtle shifts in power. We also examined the differences between manipulation, coercion and influencing and considered a useful five-step model to improve our influencing skills. We then moved onto transactional analysis and its role in communication. Finally, we learnt some tips on dealing with powerful people, and how to empower ourselves and others in order to promote co-operative power in the workplace.

9

Dealing with emotions

Most executives have a notoriously underdeveloped capacity for understanding and dealing with emotions.

(Manfred Kets de Vries, INSEAD, France)

In this chapter we explore the role of emotions in conflict and emphasize the importance of acknowledging and expressing our feelings. We examine some of the more difficult emotions to deal with, both our own and others, and examine how to handle anger.

Identifying our emotions

Conflicts are caused by emotions. They do not involve clear, logical, sequential thinking. They are not cerebral. They are concerned with our feelings – heart, not head.

Some of us have an instinctive dislike of talking about feelings – the phrase 'touchy-feely-weepy' is often used in a derogatory manner. Real people do not show their feelings, they move on.

And yet it is now proposed that 'emotional intelligence' may be as important as, if not more important than, the better known intelligence quotient (IQ) indicators in measuring a person's ability to succeed in the world.

Recently reported phenomena such as road rage, phone rage, air rage, running amok, shooting, stabbing and so on, are one indication of the level of emotional illiteracy in many societies today.

Emotional intelligence comprises an ability to motivate oneself and persist in the face of frustrations; to control impulse and delay gratification; to regulate one's moods and keep distress from swamping the ability to think, to empathize and to hope (Goleman, 1995). Emotionally intelligent people are able to recognize and acknowledge their feelings and to choose how to respond. We cannot choose our emotions, but we can choose what to do with them.

Exercise

Remember a time when someone made you feel angry, sad or frustrated. Remember all the details of that encounter and what you felt at the time. Where are you physically feeling the tension right now?

In workshops, participants report tension in one or more of the following parts of the body: the head, neck, jaw, back, stomach, calves. You may feel it somewhere else. Emotions cause physical reactions and these are stored in your body if they are not released in a healthy and positive manner.

Now, if you are sitting, stand up from your chair, move around the room and shake to rid yourself of the tension in your body.

Conflict and your emotions

Our emotions are often the main stumbling block in our attempts to be rational and logical. An emotion is a state of feeling with physiological and cognitive aspects. Although emotions are also intensely private matters, we cannot keep them entirely to ourselves. Our facial expressions and physiological reactions usually betray us.

Many emotions are universally recognized. Charles Darwin, the originator of the theory of evolution, believed that recognizing facial expressions had a survival value. For example, recognizing the signs of anger could alert us to danger even in the absence of a common language.

Some of the most common emotions associated with conflict are anger, fear, resentment, guilt, hurt and regret. These emotions are likely to impede our reasoning powers and prevent satisfactory management of conflict. Let us examine each of these emotions more closely.

Anger

Expressing anger can be a positive step towards resolving conflict. Aristotle said: 'Anyone can become angry – that is easy. But to be angry with the right person, to the right degree, at the right time, for the right purposes and in the right way – this is not easy.' If anger is appropriately expressed, then it is healthy. If not, then the results can be tragic – for example, the Hungerford massacre or the Dunblane shootings.

Fear

There are different levels of fear that may arise when we feel out of control in a conflict and we cannot predict the outcome. Some people fear showing anger: 'What if I lose my job?' 'Suppose he never forgives me?' When this occurs we need to face up to the fear. Fears are often irrational and once we think of the worst that can happen, we may find it is not as bad as we thought. Justified fears need to be thought out and a contingency plan put in place. Carry out a risk assessment and plan what you will do in the event of a negative consequence.

Resentment

Described as frozen anger, resentment eats away at us, influencing our every judgement. When we resent someone, we foster self-righteousness, envy and 'victim' behaviour. It is much easier to resent someone than to take responsibility for our own behaviour. Resentments also stockpile. If we do not deal with resentment initially, it will colour every new conflict and we become unable to differentiate between current issues and 'old baggage'.

Guilt

Conflict can often leave us feeling guilty. Were we too harsh? Could we have dealt with it in another manner? Guilt can be a learning factor if we acknowledge our feelings and take action, for example, apologizing or otherwise trying to resolve the matter. Often, though, we live with the guilt until it is too late to do anything about it.

Hurt

Words have a terrible ability to wound and when we are in the grip of emotions, we often say things we would prefer to have remained unsaid. The hurt remains and words spoken cannot then be unspoken. Acknowledging that we are hurt is important, otherwise hurt can fossilize into resentment.

Regret

One of the saddest phrases is 'if only'. If we only knew what lay ahead, what would we have done instead. Feeling regret for our part in a conflict can motivate us to take action. If we only feel regret and do nothing about it, then we are encouraging negative emotions that simply sap our energy.

Exercise

On a scale of 1 to 10, how do you feel today? Can you find the exact adjective to describe how you feel? Do you feel happy or sad? Contented or frustrated? Tense or relaxed?

Recognizing how we feel is the foundation of emotional literacy. If we habitually exaggerate (awfulize) or dilute our emotions, we will never be able to control them; they will control us, with all the possible consequences.

You can hear the mislabelling of emotions on a regular basis if you listen to the media. People consider themselves to be 'gutted' and 'devastated' over the most trivial of events. When faced with genuine tragedy, they are too overwhelmed to cope. Recognizing our feelings on a regular basis is a discipline that becomes easier as we go along.

Focusing and labelling

Have you ever had a 'name on the tip of your tongue' that you simply cannot remember? The harder you try, the more difficult it becomes. Suddenly, out of the blue, the answer comes to us. Can you recall the immense relief when you finally remember? You probably moved your body and let out a great sigh of relief. It is as if that forgotten name has actually been taking up space inside your body, causing tension and discomfort, and now by remembering the name we have liberated that space and we feel lighter and more comfortable.

Emotions that are not expressed remain in your body causing muscular tension and rigidity. Some researchers attribute a large number of illnesses and diseases to unexpressed emotion and stress. This is why some people cry when a particularly knotted muscle is manipulated through massage. The stored emotions are released together with the muscular tension.

Exercise

Find a quiet spot where you can concentrate and will not be interrupted. Think of an event that particularly affected you. If you cannot bring one to mind straight away, consider any news item that particularly moved you: for example, a famine in Africa; a natural disaster; or a local crime about which you have a strong opinion.

Ask yourself how you feel about it – you will probably need to test a number of adjectives, or labels, until you find the right one. For example, you might start with 'angry'. You may be surprised to find that it does not convey your exact feelings. You try again, 'furious', that still does not fit. Suddenly, the word 'powerless' flits across your mind. You will know that you have 'hit the spot' when your body shifts, you experience an emotional release and you probably sigh and say 'That's it. That's exactly how I am feeling'.

Once you know how you are feeling, you can begin to do something about it. You may find yourself saying something like 'Right. I now acknowledge that I resent Jane's promotion. What am I going to do about it?' You will be surprised at the sense of power and control you experience just from being able to label your own feelings. Some people confuse recognizing feelings with expressing them. Emotions can be expressed in many ways: music, art, dance, drama and so on. You need to label what it is you are expressing.

Soon, you will find that you know intuitively how you are feeling most of the time. For example, if you are talking to a difficult client and you realize that you are starting to feel short tempered, you can take counter-measures to make sure you keep your temper under control.

Some people find exceptional difficulty with this exercise. They have never given their feelings much thought, and they experience discomfort in even trying. It is contrary to everything they have ever been taught. If this is the case, it is even more important to persevere. An emotionally literate society is a more civilized and peaceful one.

Labelling our feelings also extends our awareness and enriches our life experiences. There will be times when we may not find the word that adequately describes the subtlety or intensity of a particular emotion. The constant quest to find appropriate words often results in creative new turns of speech – words such as 'laid-back', 'groovy' and 'zapped' then take their place in our vocabulary.

Everything in moderation, though. What sad human beings we would be if we labelled everything we felt, forgetting to experience its richness and diversity. The management of emotions in conflict is mainly concerned with negative feelings and understanding exactly what is bothering us. We should not extend it to labelling every fleeting joyful emotion as it engulfs us, otherwise we intellectualize all our feelings and become rather boring and robotic.

Focusing on a problem or a conflict

When you have practised recognizing and labelling feelings, you will find it much easier to focus on problems. Sometimes, we mull over things, feeling vaguely troubled but unable to define exactly what is troubling us. Find a place where you can think without interruption for a while. Bring to mind the issue and ask yourself, aloud, one or more of these questions: 'What exactly is troubling me?' 'What am I sensing here?' 'What is the matter?'

Do not force yourself to think about the answer – just let your mind do the searching for you and observe what it brings up. Sometimes, you may have thoughts that seem totally irrelevant. Stick with them. They are leading you somewhere. If at the end of your allotted time, you have still not ascertained what is troubling you, let it go for now and resolve to have some answer within the next 24 hours. In more cases than not, the answer will suddenly come to you when you are least expecting it.

Expressing our emotions

Imagine that you have a tightly lidded pan full of water on the boil. If you leave it boiling furiously, you will probably notice that the pressure starts to push the lid off allowing water to seep over the sides, and then, when the pressure rises too much, it may blow the lid off completely.

Our emotions are exactly the same. If they bubble away furiously inside us, without a safe outlet, they will start to seep out, possibly in a physical sense, such as skin rashes, or verbally, with biting or sarcastic comments, and then finally they will erupt out of control – the classical 'running amok'.

We can express our emotions positively or we can express them negatively (Table 9.1).

Table 9.1 Expression of emotions

Positive expression of emotions	Negative expression of emotions
Talking/writing it out	Losing our temper
Working it off at the gym or other sport	Physical and verbal abuse
Taking a long walk	Throwing/kicking things
Meditating/focusing	Acts of sabotage or revenge
Painting, music, writing, acting	Harming ourselves (cutting)

With positive expression, we are in control and hold the balance of power. With negative expression we become out of control and give our power away.

If we do suppress or deny our emotions, we put at risk both our physical and our mental health. Nor can we continue to suppress them indefinitely. Like the pot on the boil, sooner or later we will explode. Then we will vent our feelings – probably at the wrong person!

Of course, there are times when it may be inappropriate to express your emotions, or you may want to find out more or strengthen your resources first before doing so. This is different from suppression. You have acknowledged your feelings and have taken a deliberate decision to bide your time. You are containing your feelings for the time being (Figure 9.1).

We are frequently told how healthy it is to express anger. But there is an appropriate way of doing so and an inappropriate way. Appropriate expression consists of expressing how we feel without blaming, focusing on the issue not the person and choosing the right place and the right moment.

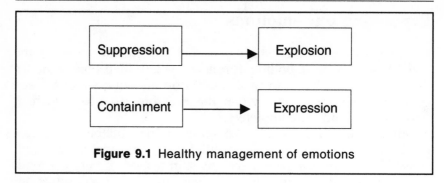

Figure 9.1 Healthy management of emotions

Centring

Can you remember a time when your body, mind and spirit seemed to be in total balance and you felt an inner peace and connection with the world around you? We have all experienced this quality of being centred at some point, even if we have not consciously recognized it. It is a very powerful feeling.

Imagine that you are looking at a large solid old tree. It has been there for centuries, its roots deep in the earth and its branches reaching up to the skies high above. Somehow the tree feels familiar and very much a part of everything around it. You could never imagine it apologizing for its existence or worrying if it was in the right place at the right time. It is a noble creation. It demands respect. Keep the image of that tree in your mind.

Through a very simple exercise, we can re-create a centred feeling in ourselves. Our bodies and our minds are one. If our mind is sad, our body is sad and if our body is tense, our mind is tense. If you do not feel grounded, if you feel 'wobbly', your mind will be the same and you are more likely to be prey to negative emotions.

Exercise

You will need a partner to re-create this. Explain to him or her what you are going to do before you start.

Ask your partner to stand at ease, feet shoulder width apart. Knees should be unlocked and the back and neck straight. He or she should lift both shoulders up and down gently a few times to relax. Ask him or her to take a deep breath in and then let it out gently and slowly.

Stand beside your partner, facing in the same direction. Gently and respectfully put the fingertips of your hand just above your partner's chest. Keep the other hand behind him or her for reassurance. Slowly and smoothly increase the pressure as if you are trying to push your partner directly back. Ask your partner not to physically resist the pressure and notice how soon he or she begins to wobble. Is it not interesting how we often describe people who are non-assertive as 'pushovers'?

Keep your fingers in the same position on your partner's chest and now ask your partner to concentrate on his or her physical centre of the body. This is roughly two inches below the navel. Have your partner locate this with a finger and then concentrate on it. You may like to suggest the image of the solid, old tree, asking him or her to imagine that their roots go deep into the earth.

Slowly increase the pressure again, while asking your partner to continue concentrating on his or her centre. Notice how much more stable your partner is. There is a relaxed resistance to the pressure and very little wobble.

Now ask your partner to do the same to you. Concentrate each time on how it feels to be centred. Once you are familiar with the feeling, you can re-create it anywhere at will – seated, lying down or standing. You can summon up the feeling of being grounded, of being centred.

Next time you feel your temper rising, or tears pricking the back of your eyes, or your throat tightening, immediately say to yourself 'Centre', take the focus of your concentration down to the spot two inches below your navel and feel the calm strength flow through your body. Take a deep breath and release any negative energy.

You may find the idea of centring alien yet a healthy living being – animal, plant or human – is naturally centred. Centring is a technique used in many martial arts, as well as yoga and meditation. Some of us live so much in the mind that we have lost touch with our body. And we have grown so accustomed to being out of touch that we become intensely uncomfortable when reminded of this fact.

Thomas Crum (1987, p. 60) tells us: 'When a person chooses that centred state, the environment around him literally feels the positive influence.'

Handling our own anger

There are times when we feel so angry that we just over react. We 'blow a gasket'.

Jack's story

It was a steaming August day and I'd had a tough time at work that had left me furious. My wife then rang and asked if I could collect some items from the supermarket on the way home. It was the last thing I felt like doing but I drove to the supermarket anyway. I couldn't find everything she wanted and then got stuck in a long queue at the checkout. When I finally returned to the car, some idiot had parked his car right up against my door so I couldn't open it. I had to get in the passenger side and cross over feeling very embarrassed and banging myself to boot. When I backed out the car and was ready to leave, I jumped out and furiously scratched along the side of his car with my car key before driving off.

Jack's story is not untypical. Our anger mounts over a period of time and because we have not expressed it appropriately, we explode and vent it on the wrong person.

It is one of life's myths that becoming aggressively angry is good for releasing our emotions. In fact, hostile people, those who are quick to anger, are more likely to suffer from cardiac disease. Managing our anger needs to be part of our lifestyle management. This includes managing stress through diet, exercise, sleep and leisure pursuits. Balancing our domestic and working lives is another vital element. Excessive stress is often caused by an imbalance somewhere in our lives.

Anger management strategies

1. *Acknowledge that you feel angry.* Take control of the emotion. This gives you time to think about your response rather than blindly reacting.
2. *Accept responsibility for your own anger.* Avoid the phrase 'he/she/they make me angry'. Nobody can make you angry. You make yourself angry.
3. *Give yourself space.* If you feel you are about to lose your temper, move yourself physically. Even a few moments on your own will cool you down sufficiently to regain control.
4. *Centre yourself.* The adult equivalent of counting from 1 to 10. Take a moment to centre and get in touch with your self.
5. *Use a tension release technique.* If you feel very angry and tense, you may benefit from releasing your anger physically in private. Go somewhere where you can be on your own and:

a) pummel or throw a pillow
b) 'strangle' a towel
c) do a 'gorilla' (jumping up and down and shouting loudly)
d) hit your palm with your fist.
e) shout, yell or scream; if you are worried about being heard, yell into a pillow
f) if you have a newspaper handy, tear up the pages and crumple them up with as much noise as you can.

You may have your own favourites. Try to avoid breaking or throwing valuables as you'll probably only regret it later.

6. *Practise deep breathing or other relaxation techniques.* Breathe in to the count of three and out to the count of six slowly for a few minutes. Exhalation triggers relaxation. By breathing out twice as slowly as breathing in, you are strengthening your relaxation response.

Have you ever heard a smoker tell you how smoking relieves their tension? Watch their breathing. First they inhale deeply then they exhale slowly, savouring the moment. In fact, they could probably gain the same relaxation benefits by simply inhaling and exhaling deeply without the aid of a cigarette. Much healthier, more socially conscious and more economical!

Use alternate nostril techniques. Close one nostril, breathe in through the other, then release the closed nostril and breathe out through that one. Alternate one nostril then another.

Use deep muscle relaxation techniques. There are many books and tapes on the market to teach these techniques or you might prefer to consult a stress therapist who could coach you.

7. *Separate the person from the problem.* By depersonalizing your anger, you can look at it more objectively. What is at stake here and how can we deal with it?

8. *Concentrate on the current issue.* Do not muddy the waters by bringing up old issues or resentments. Once this current anger has passed, address 'old baggage' separately.

Handling difficult emotions in others

Return briefly to the difficult emotions we mentioned earlier on (anger, fear, resentment, guilt, hurt and regret). Faced with another person displaying some of these emotions, we often feel embarrassed, impatient or simply powerless. Our reactions will depend on our rapport with the other person. If we have established a close relationship, it will be easier to deal with the situation. Our objective is to bring the emotional temperature down to a level where a constructive dialogue can ensue.

When we are the butt of someone's intense emotions, we often react defensively. This is especially so if an angry confrontation was not expected or we were taken by surprise. The other common reaction is simply to feel sorry for ourselves and switch into 'victim' mode. Anger and fear often go together. People may feel too frightened to express their anger, or they may mistake fear for anger.

If you are dealing with a fearful person, then you need to help them distinguish between justified fears and irrational ones. It can be useful to help them compile a risk assessment. This can be a list of 'what is the worst that can happen?' and 'what are my contingency plans?'

Fear and guilt also go together. An employee cheating on expenses or filching stationery or stamps will feel guilty and afraid of being found out. There is also another type of irrational guilt. For example, someone who received a promotion you wanted or who was chosen to go on a training course you wanted to go on may feel guilty.

Resentment can create feelings of guilt in others. Are you dealing with someone who resents you? Working with resentful colleagues can be hard. Resentment affects motivation and morale of everyone around them and creates a 'them and us' atmosphere. Resentful people are often more difficult to deal with than angry people as they tend to withdraw into themselves and maintain a wall of silence.

Hurt people, too, often withdraw into themselves and refuse to be part of the working environment. Their lack of communication can destroy team spirit.

We do not arrive in this world with an instruction manual on how to be handled. And even if we did, few of us would bother to read the instructions until 'all else had failed'. People are different, emotions are individual and circumstances vary widely. There is no universal prescription, no magic formula.

If, however, we learn to reflect after every difficult encounter, we can begin to gain a feel for what generally works and what does not. In addition, we need to take into account current political and social climates. Actions or words that were once *de rigueur* are frowned upon. Political correctness may dictate what we can or cannot say or do. For example, physical touch is a vexatious question. It is an intensely personal choice. Do you or don't you?

Touching people who are highly emotional may cause them to lose their final grip on themselves. This can lead to distressing behaviour such as loud sobs, hyperventilation, and other extreme reactions. When the person is fully back in control, he or she will probably be twice as mortified.

The other reason for avoiding touch is that when emotions run high and a person is confused, he or she may accuse you of sexual harassment. At work, it is better to be safe than sorry and the benefit of a touch may be outweighed by other considerations.

Dealing with tears

People in the grip of any strong emotion, including anger, may also dissolve into tears when confronted. This can be difficult to deal with at the best of times but when it happens in an office, the tearful person may also have to deal with feelings of inadequacy and lack of professionalism. Particularly, if a manager breaks down in front of those he or she is managing.

1. Acknowledge the tears matter of factly. 'I can see you're upset now'.
2. Match the other person's body position but do not make physical contact. For example, if the person is standing, stand up beside them or if you are sitting and there is a chair available, invite them to sit down. Place yourself beside the person rather than facing them straight on. This increases empathy and is less threatening.
3. Remain silent for a few moments. Breathe slowly and evenly. This often helps to calm the other person.
4. When you feel the moment is right, you can make an empathetic but neutral comment, for example, 'Sometimes things get on top of us, don't they?' or 'You're not having the easiest of days, are you?' This will usually elicit some sort of response that you can build on.
5. If the other person wants to speak, then just listen. If he or she demonstrates a desire to be on their own, respect that and let them know you are available to talk later, if they want to.
6. Do not offer tissues and cups of tea. The less fuss you make the better. If the person needs a tissue and you have one, hand it over without comment. If the person wants to talk, you can suggest a cup of tea or coffee but only if you have someone who can bring it in to you. Do not leave the room as this will break the rapport.

Handling an angry outburst

The goal in handling an angry outburst is not to resolve the conflict there and then but to keep the situation on an even keel and protect your own physical and psychological space.

1. *Check your mindchatter.* We have already seen the effect of 'reacting' rather than 'responding'. An angry person can lead us to jump into defensive patterns of behaviour and escalate the situation. We need to break this pattern by superimposing new and more positive thoughts. Begin by acknowledging your habitual reactions and then use some positive self-talk to overcome them. For example:
   a) 'An angry person is out of control. I am in control. Therefore, the balance of power lies with me.'
   b) 'People often say things they don't mean when they are angry.'
   c) 'I can repair the damage to my self-esteem later on.'
   d) 'This person is probably dumping their anger on me by mistake.'
   e) 'This person must be under a lot of stress.'
   f) 'Tell me where it's written that life should be fair.'
   Use these as starting-points to your own affirmations. Above all, this is not a theoretical exercise. Remember to use them when faced with anger.
2. *Centre yourself.* Concentrate on your body for a few moments and ensure that you are not holding any excessive tension anywhere. Your aim is a state of relaxed alertness. This will ensure that the right signals go to your brain to prepare you for the verbal onslaught or even physical attack.
3. *Check your body position.* Match the other person's level so you are not at a physical disadvantage. Remember that having to look up to or down at someone can be threatening or intimidating. If an angry person is standing, stand up. If he or she is sitting, change your body posture to a more upright sitting position. This should deter him or her from standing as there is less physical threat from a seated person.
   Watch your body space. Each of you needs plenty of space around you and you may need to take a discreet step backwards if the other person invades your own personal space. This should be done very casually otherwise it may be interpreted as fear.
   Try to stand or sit on the same side as the other person, both facing the same direction. Psychologically, that creates a

feeling of 'we are both in this together and the problem is out there' rather than facing each other with the implication that the problem is between you – or even is part of you.

If, however, you are faced with an out of control or potentially violent situation, then you need to put a barrier between you. A desk or chair will do. You should also note where the door is so that you can exit easily, if necessary.

If your job does carry the risk of physical violence, acquaint yourself with the specific guidelines laid down by your health and safety executive and follow these to the letter.

4. *Listen and receive.* An angry person is not receptive to logic and will not listen to you. There is no point in trying to reason with him or her. In fact, you will only make matters worse if you do. Acknowledge the other person's feelings: 'You are obviously very angry' or 'I can understand that you are annoyed' or 'I can see that you are very concerned about this matter'. Use a calm and serious tone of voice.

It may be appropriate to use an 'I' statement to express your own emotions, for example, 'I feel the situation is spiralling out of control', 'I feel like postponing this discussion till later' or 'I feel upset that things have reached this far'. (For a more detailed treatment see Cornelius and Faire, 1989, pp. 51–3.)

5. *Use active listening techniques.* Reflect back what the person is saying to you in your own words: 'So what you are saying is that...' or 'Let me check if I have understood this correctly. You feel that...'

6. *Make a peace offering.* Sometimes, just showing willingness to resolve or offering a gesture of conciliation will stop the aggression. The attacker may do so reluctantly or with bad grace but even that is better than the continued abuse. You may wish to consider:
   a) an apology
   b) an acknowledgement of the other person's needs
   c) an acceptance of your own part in the problem
   d) recognition that the other person has a right to be angry
   e) a genuine attempt to bring the matter to a positive resolution.

7. *Transforming dispute into dialogue.* Once the person has calmed down, look at each party's needs and concerns. Often what happens is a statement of positions instead of a genuine attempt to understand the other's point of view. Both parties need to move forward with the issue and become solution focused.

Dealing with backstabbers, and saboteurs

1. *Acknowledge what is happening.* You usually know when someone is out to harm you. They will try to bring you into disrepute or to make you look foolish, unprofessional or incompetent. This can be achieved by public humiliation, sniping or calculated manipulation. It can be subtle or an all-out war.

   Whatever the case may be, you need to confront the issue. Ignoring it or pretending that it does not matter will not work. You will probably be seen as weak and there is a danger that others will join in with the perpetrator and see you as 'fair game'.

2. *Revise your own attitude.* This is paramount, and the attitude you wish to develop is one of amused curiosity. It helps to repeat to yourself 'How fascinating'. This puts the behaviour into perspective and keeps you mentally tough.

   Some people are simply 'jokers'. They are insensitive and often not too bright, and may not realize that they are causing such offence or even distress. If so, simply tell them how you feel and ask them to desist in their behaviour. If they do not, then you need to consider that they are doing it on purpose and move on to other tactics.

3. *Respond immediately.* Let us say you are in a meeting and the offender makes a sarcastic comment that reflects on your professionalism or ability, you need to deal with it publicly there and then. If you are talking, interrupt yourself and if someone else has started talking, ask if you may just deal with the comment before continuing proceedings. Do not think that others will not have noticed sarcasm or sniping. You will be respected for dealing with the matter assertively and non-emotionally.

Your attacker may have used a non-verbal weapon such as a facial gesture or expression denoting disapproval or a put-down. If you are in the middle of a sentence, complete what you were saying calmly and then turn to the other person saying something like, 'I can see you disagree with what I have just said. I'd like to hear your opinion.'

If the comment was made in an aside to someone else (a saboteur's favourite method!) then you can say something like, 'I didn't quite catch what you said there. Could you tell the whole group?' The object here is not so much to make the person repeat what was said but to ensure that he or she knows that you are aware of the sniping and to bring it to the attention of all present.

Occasionally, a comment will be openly demeaning or condescending. For example, 'I know you're new to the job and you can't be expected to understand the whole issue but...' or 'That's typical of an MBA virgin'. There is no point in entering into a slanging match with this sort of comment. You will win respect by saying something like, 'What are you really trying to say?' or 'I'm not sure I understand your intention'.

Uncover any hidden agendas privately. Try to get to the bottom of what is happening with an opening statement such as, 'I'm not too sure what is going on here and I'd really like to resolve it and work together as a team' or 'I'm feeling uncomfortable about our working relationship and would like to clear the air'. Then listen, listen, listen. Only then can you try to solve the problem.

The secret of dealing with difficult people is to remember that they normally think you are the problem. Once you show them that you are cooperative, most people will respond in a reasonable manner.

Be aware, however, that there is a small core of totally unreasonable people, for example, serial bullies, who are genuinely devious, divisive and spiteful. If you are unlucky enough to be involved with a boss or co-worker who displays such tendencies then you will need to take further advice.

Summary

The focus of our attention in this chapter was on how we handle our own emotions during conflict. To achieve this, we discussed labelling our emotions and recognizing our reactions to them. When we can manage our own emotions successfully, we can move on to managing others' difficult emotions. We examined positive and negative methods of releasing emotions and examined what happens when we hold on to negative emotions instead of releasing them in a healthy manner. Finally, we considered ways of dealing with two particularly difficult emotions: tears and anger.

10

Overcoming reluctance

There is no shame in being wrong, only in failing to correct our mistakes.

(George Soros, 1930, investor)

You may have heard the old joke 'How many therapists does it require to change a light bulb?' 'One. But first the light bulb must be willing to change.'

I have always found that joke particularly significant when related to conflict. With all the techniques in the world, no conflict will ever be resolved unless there is, first, a willingness to resolve it. This chapter looks at our own part in a conflict and our own willingness to resolve matters.

Why are we often so unwilling to resolve a conflict?

Exercise

Cast your mind back to a conflict that you, personally, were unwilling to resolve. What were your reasons for not wanting to resolve the matter?

Here are some possible explanations (or excuses):

- 'Because I was right (and the other person was wrong).'
- 'Because the other person really upset me.'
- 'Because I was treated unfairly.'
- 'Because I cut them out of my life.'
- 'Because the other person really didn't matter.'
- 'My pride wouldn't let me.'
- 'Because I felt it would make things worse to discuss it.'
- 'I wouldn't apologize on principle.'
- 'Because they owe me an apology.'
- 'Because I wanted to teach the other person a lesson.'

There may be possible short-term benefits to us if we leave a conflict unresolved:

- We do not need to admit our own part in it.
- We do not risk rejection or humiliation.
- We do not reopen old wounds.
- We can maintain our self-righteousness.
- We can continue to convince ourselves that we were right.
- Resentment may sometimes give certain people a focus in life.
- We may enjoy the drama.

You may have heard yourself say 'I'm willing to reconsider if they apologize' or 'I'll forget about it if they admit they are wrong'. Remember, the other party is feeling exactly the same way and saying exactly the same thing. We stand on opposite sides of the wall, unwilling to budge an inch till the other takes the first step. We refuse to concede and we refuse to apologize.

However, it takes two to tango, and we have already seen how behaviour breeds behaviour. A continuing conflict is shared energy. If one withdraws or disengages then the dynamics of the conflict inevitably change in some way.

> *Change begins with me.*

US President Harry Truman allegedly had a notice on his desk saying 'The buck stops here'. We, too, can express the same sentiment and take responsibility for our part in the conflict.

Let us consider a conflict that we resolved to our satisfaction. What benefits did we gain?

- A deeper understanding of the other person/issue.
- A sense of relief.
- Pride in our abilities.
- Enhanced self-esteem.
- A new perspective on life.
- Understanding someone else's point of view.
- More experience.
- Enhanced interpersonal communication skills.
- Renewed or deepened friendship.

It would appear then that there are many benefits from resolving conflict in return for the possible temporary discomfort in making the first move. It does require some moral courage to face an unknown situation that could considerably challenge our comfort zones. Psychologists reveal that we human beings like to stay within our comfort zones and resist moving outside their limits. Truly, the only thing that holds us back is our own lack of confidence and unwillingness to risk failure or rejection.

Let us examine our own unwillingness to resolve a conflict. To reach out and make the first move, we need to be introspective and think about those areas of our lives and our consciences that we would rather avoid.

We can refuse to take a long hard look at what is actually happening. We may feel that if we ignore it, it will eventually go away. If we look back at the levels of conflict, we will see that conflicts rarely disappear. They may disappear for a while, or they may plateau out at one of the levels for a time, only to re-emerge with renewed hostility at a later date.

Richard's story

I had a very good job as a marketing manager in the travel industry. I loved my job and believe I was very competent at what I did. I never liked my Marketing Director. I spent as little time as possible with him and tried to avoid any social contact. Yes, I did moan about him to my colleagues and also to other industry people at conferences, exhibitions and other events. It reached the point where it was impossible to ignore the tension any longer. We were not sniping openly at each other, but we managed to build up two camps in the office nevertheless. We seemed to be fighting battles all the time, scoring points off each other, until one day it dawned on me that I was going to lose the war eventually. I gave in my notice and moved to another company. I was happy there for 18 months until my current boss moved on. His post was advertised and I applied. Unbeknown to me, my ex-boss also applied and he got the job. After all this time, I was back to square one again. I bitterly regretted not having made some attempt to resolve the matter between us in our previous employment.

Many people I have spoken to tell the same tale. Sooner or later, old rivals or enemies reappear in their lives, often in positions of authority. It hardly ever makes sense to leave a company on bad terms with a boss or colleague. You may have heard the saying 'Always be kind to people on your way up, because you never know where you will meet them again on the way down'.

Do you know anyone who irritates you beyond reason and to whom you react irrationally? It could be somebody you know or someone in the public eye. If you have never reacted in this manner, can you think of another person who does, while you remain bemused by all the fuss? 'What on earth is it about James that drives Sue to distraction?', you'll think. 'He seems a harmless enough fellow to me.' But, of course, you are not Sue.

Why do we perceive things so differently? Why do we react differently? This is a problem the police often face when examining witnesses. They could have three people who saw exactly the same incident, each recounting a different version. And each would swear that their version is correct and others are wrong.

An old but still dramatic test is that of presenting a group with an ambiguous picture. Some people will see one thing and others will see something completely different.

Look at the picture in Figure 10.1. What do you see? Do you see an old woman or a young woman? Or do you see them both? If you see them both, notice that you have to mentally adjust your thinking and your focus to switch from seeing the old woman to the young, and vice versa.

What happens here is that we experience the lock-in/lock-out syndrome. When we first see something we 'lock into' the first picture or explanation and therefore 'lock out' any other interpretations or possibilities. This is a very common and, indeed, natural occurrence. Our brains are designed to simplify and generalize so once we see something that we can accept, we no longer need to look for alternatives.

To take this a step further, we will often regard a situation from our point of view, 'lock into' our interpretation and produce

Figure 10.1 An ambiguous drawing
Source: After Boring (1930).

a solution which cannot possibly be acceptable to the other party since their interpretation of the matter is so dramatically different from our own. We also tend to look for solutions before we have even properly defined the problem.

We have also established that two parties can look at exactly the same picture and see two very different issues. We view things through different lenses. A great deal of research has been carried out on cross-gender communication, for example, and which has been popularized by writers such as Deborah Tannen (1990; 1992) and John Gray (1993). We often think we know why we disagree with another person since we look for the obvious, such as culture, religion, values etc. But there is also another aspect known as projection.

The Swiss psychologist Carl Jung presented an interesting theory on our personalities. In it he describes our personalities as containing two halves, as shown in Figure 10.2.

The top half of the figure is our persona, which is Greek for an actor's mask. This is our self-image. The other half is our shadow personality, containing aspects of our personality, both good and bad, that we do not acknowledge. In here lurk unconscious desires, past suppressed experiences, and other issues not consciously acknowledged and dealt with.

It is understandably difficult for us to acknowledge undesirable aspects in our personality, but equally we may be denying hidden talents, creative tendencies or even flashes of genius that we are not ready to acknowledge. Once these have been brought out into the open and dealt with, they become part of our persona and thus our shadow reduces in size.

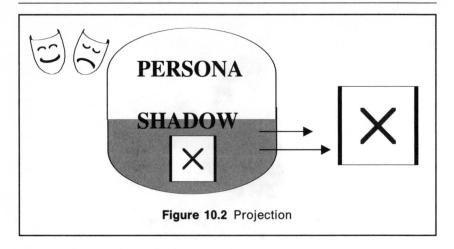

Figure 10.2 Projection

Recognizing what lies in our shadow can help us understand why we may be unwilling to resolve a continuing conflict or, indeed, stoke the fires even further.

Consider the irritating person you earlier identified. They are likely to elicit the phrase 'He or she makes me so angry' and you become emotionally engaged. It is almost as if they hook you in, like a fish on the end of a reel. What is happening here?

One of the most likely explanations is that you are experiencing 'projection', which means projecting our own unacceptable characteristics on to others. Examples can include a sexually repressed person who interprets every innocent gesture as a sexual advance or an older worker who puts every problem down to ageism. When we become unreasonably inflamed about something or someone, the cause is often in us. It may well be an indicator that we are caught up in projection.

Jane's story

> When Caroline joined our company as head of the Public Relations Department, I took an instant dislike to her. She was attractive, extrovert and the centre of attention wherever she went. I was convinced that she regarded me as a threat and am embarrassed to admit how often I sniped at her and made malicious comments behind her back. She was always so pleasant to me and I had no cause to dislike her so much. It was only when I learned about projection that I admitted to myself that I was envious of her. She reminded me of my younger sister who was pretty, vivacious and

popular – all the things I was not and had always
longed to be.

Once I accepted that Caroline was not actually the
cause but part of my projection, I began to accept my
emotions and to find a way of dealing with them. I
asked Caroline out for lunch and apologized for my
unreasonable behaviour. I also asked if she would
become my mentor and help me move into her field. I
made it clear that I was not about to sabotage her job
or her security with the firm. I simply wanted her help
in moving up. I couldn't have found a better mentor.
We became firm friends and she helped me secure a
junior job in public relations elsewhere. I have since
become a manager and am mentoring one of our more
ambitious secretaries. If she makes it in the business,
nobody will be happier and prouder than me.

There are three possible areas that could result in projection (for a
more detailed explanation see Cornelius and Faire, 1989, pp. 110–
12):

1. *Unfinished business or personal baggage.* This is what we are left
   with if we do not conclude matters satisfactorily. For example,
   you may have been in a relationship that turned sour with
   your partner terminating it by simply moving on without
   explanation. Your need to understand and to come to terms
   with the loss has never been met. If you later meet someone
   who, somehow, reminds you of your previous partner, you
   are likely to overreact. You carry your baggage around with
   you from relationship to relationship, unloading it on one
   person after another.

   Unresolved personal history can often bog us down in the
   murky mire of childhood and the 'Let's blame our parents'
   type of thinking. Blaming parents or anyone else does not
   help. Realize that the common factor is you and examine your
   own part in such relationships.
2. *Suppressed needs.* There are many reasons why we might suppress a need. It could be because we do not want to acknowledge it or we are afraid of what would happen whether it is
   fulfilled or not.

   We may have a relationship that is mostly satisfactory but
   not fulfilling particular needs. We feel guilty and thus suppress them. During our upbringing we are often rebuked for
   expressing our needs: 'You ungrateful child, you don't know

how lucky you are' or 'We've given you everything you could possibly want and you now want to chuck it all away on a whim' and so on. If we see someone who has achieved what we wanted, then we may become angry or resent him or her.

3. *Unacknowledged or unacceptable characteristics.* These may be positive or negative. For example, if we are, or have ever been, dishonest, we will see dishonesty all around us. Some of the people most vocal in their criticism of prejudice or discrimination display these characteristics themselves. Because of the politically correct climate surrounding us, we feel too intimidated to speak about such matters and they thus become part of the great ocean of 'unmentionables' in which we swim. These issues are such a common cause of conflict that they need to be brought out into the open, understood and acknowledged.

The same principle applies to the unacknowledged positive qualities we own. It might suit us to deny our own strengths or positive points. Suppose I never passed an examination in my life – it might be easier for me to pass myself off as 'thick as two planks' than to admit that I simply was too lazy or too scared of failure to achieve my qualifications.

We are often reluctant to explore our inner psyche, our unconscious hidden fears and desires. In the past, I have felt reluctant to examine my failures and painful experiences because I just could not face them. I cannot be unique. Others may also prefer to suppress, ignore or tolerate certain occurrences because the alternative of delving into our painful realities is just too difficult.

If you feel unable to confront certain issues at this point in your life, however, at least accept the concept that part of the problem may lie within you. Then you have been more than repaid for the cost of this book.

Exercise

Choose one person with whom you have a troubled relationship. Describe the qualities, attitudes or behaviours that you find difficult to deal with. How do you normally react to this person? How do you feel when you are with them? Why do you feel this way? Concentrate on yourself and your own part in the relationship, paying particular attention to possible issues residing in your shadow.

Now see if you can complete this sentence (this is an exercise in self-awareness and is not designed to be read by anyone else):

When (name of person) does/says _____ I feel _____ because I am projecting my own _____.

A word of caution: Discovering projection can sometimes lead to overusing it. You may find yourself unconsciously diagnosing people and wondering what they are projecting and whether what you think they are projecting is actually a figment of your own projection. Soon you can become confused and possibly even somewhat paranoid about the whole subject.

This is where a little knowledge can be a dangerous thing. The object of this exercise is simply to increase your self-awareness. It is just another avenue to be explored when we find ourselves unreasonably angry about something. It does not imply that you have to be projecting. I presented a short and oversimplified version of projection. If you want to find out more, you should refer to a more specialized psychology book.

Acknowledging others' positive qualities

This is all very well, you may be saying, so now I realize that I may be projecting something from my own personality onto the person with whom I feel uncomfortable. It has not lessened my bitterness towards them. What can I do to reduce this hostility?

Do you remember the song 'Just a spoonful of sugar helps the medicine go down'? When we have to drink something bitter we try to reduce the bitterness by adding sweeteners. The same principle applies in trying to reduce our resentment towards somebody. We need to recognize that somewhere inside that person there are some positive qualities.

When we are angry with or hostile to someone, we tend to cling to our feelings almost like a security blanket. Why do we do this?

- We feel self-righteous.
- We do not have to think too much of our own emotional responses.
- It is easier to put the entire blame on another person.
- It acts as a protective shield against intense pain, grief and hurt.

- The hormonal activity released by these negative emotions often helps us to cope initially.
- We may cling to our resentment in order to punish the other person.

While we hold on to negative emotions, we tend to paint the other person in the worst possible light. We dwell on their worst points in order to make ourselves feel better. This is a short-term pay-off and may work initially to help us get through the experience. But if we continually harbour resentment and hostility, this will eventually colour our own lives, our own attitudes and outlooks and eventually our health. Does it not make sense to rid our closet of such skeletons and start afresh?

The more positive qualities we can recognize in a person, the less intense our hostility becomes. We need to counteract our bitterness with some sweeteners. Each increase in positive recognition reduces the level of hostility.

The line in Figure 10.3 represents a continuum between hostility and recognition. The more hostility we feel towards another person, the less recognition of their good qualities we can muster up.

When we are hostile to or resentful of a person we demonize them and by recognizing their positive qualities we slowly begin to humanize them again (Figure 10.4). Each element of recognition removes one element of the demonization until they are back to being fully human again. This may be a slow process, the first good quality helps remove the demon's horns, the second removes its tail, the third miniaturizes the pitchfork and so on.

Try saying, 'I may not like Susan but she is very good on the telephone' or 'John is a pain in the neck but I must admit he is

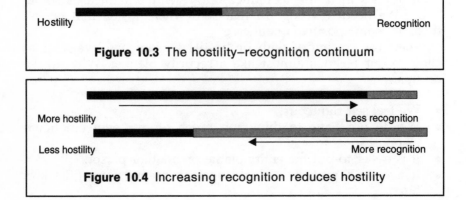

Figure 10.3 The hostility–recognition continuum

Figure 10.4 Increasing recognition reduces hostility

loyal to the company' and so on. In other words, try and find good qualities or skills in the person concerned, and somehow try to think of them in a good light.

Another way is to consider the positive intention behind their behaviour towards us. We have already examined how our mindchatter can affect our attitudes. When we are hostile to people, we tend to see their worst aspects. Then whatever they do, we say 'Well, its no more than I expected from them'. But if we were to change our belief system to presuppose that every person makes the best behavioural choice available to them at the time, how would we then view other people?

Most of us are born with enormous potential, but few of us reach our full capabilities. This may be due to an inadequate upbringing, poor education, a deprived environment or other such factors. Giving people the benefit of the doubt helps us to come to terms with bad behaviour, given their impoverished levels of knowledge, interpersonal skills and behaviour.

Some people will stop at this point and start thinking 'Here we go again! The current liberal cult of excusing the criminal and blaming the victim'. This is not the intention. If we truly believe that every person makes the best behavioural choice available to them within their own map of the world or if they have no choices or options to start with, it will help us to ignore many petty, if not serious, incidents.

Perhaps the other person has never realized that they have a behavioural choice – that they can choose to use abusive or respectful language, violence or non-violence, to cheat or to be honest. Some people genuinely do not realize that they can choose to respond rather than react. Even the lowest forms of life can react. Human beings were gifted with the ability to choose their behaviour. We can also choose to rise above others' transgressions.

What is meant by positive intention? Imagine I am walking down the street when someone appears out of the blue, mugs me and steals my handbag. Positive intention does not mean the person has a positive intention by mugging me but that the universe has a positive intention by putting me through that experience – no matter how dreadful. We will retain a more tolerant and philosophical attitude towards adversity if we believe we are put on this planet to learn from everything that happens to us.

Louise's testimony

I was a senior executive, in line and eager for a promotion to the board. However, there was one thorn in my side – a fellow executive who seemed to make it his life's mission to put me down. In public and in private, he sneered at everything I said, contradicted me on every occasion, found faults in my proposals and errors in my reports. I reached the point where I was so stressed I was making stupid mistakes and unwise decisions. My pride didn't allow me to confide in anyone at work and I pretended to take it all in my stride. When I arrived home, however, I 'hit the bottle', spending the evening trying to blot out the day's events. I finally realized that if I didn't pull myself together, I would lose my chances of promotion. I consulted a personal coach who explained the concept of positive intention. It didn't make any sense to me at all but my coach suggested I plant the seed of the idea in my head, and sleep on it.

The next morning, it suddenly struck me. 'Of course', I thought. 'This person has been sent to teach me to check my facts thoroughly, present my points clearly and succinctly and keep calm in the face of constant interrogation.' If I couldn't hold my own with this one person, how was I expected to face an entire board, some of whom would probably be just as challenging as my colleague? That was the positive intention of the behaviour. This changed my attitude. Instead of becoming defensive when he attacked me, I welcomed his comments, reframing them into a learning experience. I listened carefully, learned how to pick out underlying messages, and how to refute the argument assertively. Soon, I was actually enjoying these encounters and learnt how to hold my own in any situation. I did get my promotion to the board and my colleague left very shortly afterwards. I had no bitterness towards him at all and to this day I am thankful for what I learned.

Often we can only see the positive intention behind a painful experience retrospectively and with the benefit of hindsight. All I can suggest is that you try it. It works.

Letting go

There comes a time in our lives when we make a conscious decision to let go. This could be by forgiving another person, putting

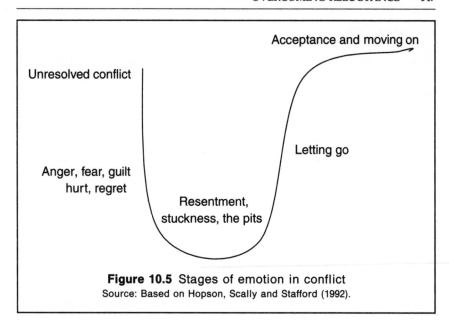

Figure 10.5 Stages of emotion in conflict
Source: Based on Hopson, Scally and Stafford (1992).

an experience behind us and getting on with our lives, or learn-ing to come to terms with the grief someone has caused us.

Moving from stuckness and resentment to letting go requires courage and motivation (Figure 10.5) – the very two qualities most lacking in an angry or resentful person. When we continue to harbour this resentment, when we remain frozen in our emo-tions, we spiral down to depression and confusion, or the pits. We have three options when we are in the pits:

1. Move back into anger and resentment.
2. Stay in the pits indefinitely.
3. Let go.

Letting go does not necessarily mean forgiving the other person. Letting go is a way of protecting our own self-esteem and mental well-being. We may decide to forgive and forget, to forgive but not to forget, or we may decide to live with the problem or to cut that person out of our lives and move on. Whatever the outcome, reaching a decision is the first decisive step and comes as an enormous relief of the stress and nervous tension that has built up inside us.

Of the three decisions outlined above, which would you choose? And if you need to do so eventually, why waste valuable living time in the pits?

Forgiveness

Why is it so very, very hard to forgive? Sometimes, the hurt and grief are so deep that we cannot forgive, no matter what we have been taught is the correct thing to do. Or we may decide to forgive and continue a relationship, but the trust has gone. Like a cracked mirror, it cannot be made brand new again so you learn to accept the cracks.

You must decide for yourself what your attitude towards the other person is going to be from now on. There is no point in saying you will forgive a person but then bring up the past with them all the time, or continuing to harbour resentment or hurt. Consider the long-term and the short-term consequences and pay-offs.

There is an Arab proverb that says when someone betrays you, do not retaliate, just wait for the universe to act for you. Although those who cheat, manipulate, and backstab may seem to thrive, it is only short term. Sooner or later, they will pay for it. In the meantime, if you learn to forgive them or at the very least let go of your resentment, you will be protecting your own self-esteem and the balance of power will lie with you.

People often say, 'This is all well and good but I am quite willing to resolve an old conflict with someone. The trouble is they are not willing to resolve it. They're not even ready to meet me halfway.' How do you know someone is unwilling to resolve? Do they

- refuse to discuss the issue?
- pretend everything is all right when you both know it's not?
- ignore you?
- say the problem is yours, not theirs?
- tell you they do not know what you are talking about, then bring it up on every occasion?
- criticize you to others?
- sabotage you at every chance?

I once had the following exchange with a colleague:

> *Colleague*: 'Well, I just know he's not willing to resolve.'
> *Me*: 'Have you actually discussed it and told him you want to resolve the matter?'
> *Colleague*: 'Not really, no. I just know he won't want to discuss it.'

Here, we are fortune telling. We are forecasting that the other person will not want to discuss it and, therefore, not make the first move ourselves. But the other person may be thinking exactly the same thing. They probably think *you* do not want, or will be unwilling, to resolve the matter.

Put yourself in the other person's shoes. Imagine that you are unwilling to resolve a conflict with a colleague:

> *Question*: 'What would it take for you to become more willing to listen?'
> *Answer*: 'Suppose he or she approached you in a friendly manner, offered an explanation, demonstrated a willingness to resolve or offered a small token of regret. Would that sway you?'
> *Question*: 'How would you both benefit from a resolution?'
> *Answer*: 'Considerably less anxiety, a better frame of mind, greater effectiveness, improved workplace morale, a new found friend.'

Now consider your response and devise a workable strategy that you can follow to resolve a conflict with someone whom you consider to be unwilling to resolve. You may wish to choose one of the following options:

1. *Make the first approach.* Tell the other person how you feel about the situation and highlight the benefits to all parties of resolving the matter. You may also wish to point out the detrimental effect of the conflict and the costs of leaving matters as they are.
2. *Put yourself in the other person's shoes.* Are there any issues you may be overlooking? Do you understand the other person's feelings, needs and concerns? Does he or she need to save face? If so, how can you help them do so? Is there a hidden agenda?
3. *Start a dialogue.* Make sure you are both 'singing from the same hymn sheet'. Is the issue absolutely clear to you both? What are both your needs and concerns? A mapping exercise can be invaluable here (see Chapter 11). Are your outcomes similar? Is it in the other person's interests to resolve the matter? Is there a benefit by holding on to the *status quo*?
4. *Evaluate your own part.* How good is my rapport with the other person? Am I projecting any of my past problems onto the conflict? Have I expressed myself assertively? Have I

listened carefully to what the other person is saying? Which part of this problem is mine and which is theirs?

5. *Consider your best alternative to non-resolution.* How will you feel if the bad feelings continue? How will this affect you? Do you need more time to step back emotionally and physically to reconsider? Do you need third party intervention? Is this a problem that requires mediation, or even grievance procedures?

If you have done everything you can, how are you going to protect your own well-being and move on? Do you need to change jobs, for instance? Would counselling help? Can you just let go and put it down to experience? Only you know what the best course of action may be. Whatever it is, do not hesitate. Take action to resolve the matter now.

Summary

In this chapter we considered the concept of willingness to resolve and moving on. It is unwise to ignore conflicts because the emotions and baggage stay with us. Often, we can only see problems from our own perspective, therefore, the starting-point is to reflect deeply on our own selves. We examined projection, our part in the conflict and recognizing the other person's positive points. We moved on to the stages of transition that we go through and the importance of letting go. Finally, we explored ways of approaching another party whom we suspect is unwilling to resolve and discovered some tactics to help us overcome their unwillingness.

Part III

The tools of conflict resolution

11

Mapping

The greatest challenge to any thinker is stating the problem in a way that will allow a solution.

(Bertrand Russell, 1872–1970, philosopher)

All conflicts are problems but not all problems are conflicts. Often, we try to find a solution when we have not fully understood the issue. When we try to resolve conflicts as if they were problems requiring a logical, rational approach, we often fail to find a solution. This is because conflicts are caused by emotions. There is no one easy answer and we need to approach the issue with a more creative, lateral thinking type approach. This is why mapping the conflict is invaluable. We are simply mapping the terrain – drawing a picture of the conflict so that we can examine the situation from all angles before getting to grips with how to resolve it.

Why do we need to map?

When you are planning a trip to unfamiliar territory, you normally consult a map. First, you will find out exactly where you are on the map. It is not much good plotting your route from Birmingham if you are starting from Southampton. Second, you will find out exactly where you want to go. 'Somewhere south-west of Aberdeen' will not do. You have to pinpoint the exact location as this may alter your choice of routes to get you there. Third, you will decide on the most suitable route. This may not be the shortest route – you may decide to go on a longer, more leisurely scenic route. On the other hand, time may be of essence – in which case you will seek the quickest and most direct route to get you there.

The map is not the territory. We are considering a representation of reality. We are examining one view of reality. It can be very useful to remember: *'Just because I see it like that, doesn't mean that's how it is.'*

Exercise

Try an experiment (inspired by an idea from Gareth Morgan, 1986). What do you see when you look at the picture in Figure 11.1? The most common response is that of a piglet – cute – a bit like 'Babe' the pig who thought it was a sheepdog.

Now view 'Babe' from another perspective for a minute:

1. How would it look to an ultra orthodox Jewish or Muslim person? (unclean animal)
2. How would it look to a butcher? (meat)
3. How would it look to a farmer? (money)
4. How would it look to a fox? (food)
5. How would it look to a painter or photographer? (light, shadow, expression, colour)
6. How would it look to another pig? (Guess!)
7. How does this pig observe all of us? Does it consider us in the same way? Would it perhaps be influenced by whether it were approached by a butcher or a painter?

Figure 11.1 How do you view this pig?

A conflict can also be approached in the same manner. How does it look to each of the parties? How does it look to an outsider? So by mapping the problem, we begin to form a picture of what this situation looks like. And perhaps seeing things which we had not previously noticed.

Mapping a conflict on your own

Use mapping to define your own thoughts about a conflict. You can only list the stakeholders' needs and concerns as you see them, so put yourself in their shoes and try to see the situation from their point of view. You will probably not recognize all needs and concerns as accurately as you would like. However, the resulting map will still give you a much clearer picture of the conflict and provide you with perspectives that you had not thought of before.

Mapping as a planning tool

Maps can also be a means of working out plans and tactics in advance, and for preparation for meetings.

Chris's story

I recently visited a training organization to discuss their possible need for my services. As part of my preparation I took ten minutes to jot down what might be the needs and concerns of a number of parties: the client contact, the organization, the secretary (with whom I could well be liaising on a day-to-day basis), the delegates who would come on courses, the delegates' organizations and, of course, myself.

As a result of this exercise I developed a deeper insight into what the customer might need from an associate trainer. Entering the meeting, I felt confident, open, calm and more willing to listen. I did not feel the need to talk too much about myself.

Moreover, although I felt fully prepared for any eventuality, 'objections' just did not come up. I had taken the time to step into my customer's 'map of the world'. This led to a spirit of cooperation and working together, rather than one of trying to 'get something out of each other'. It's almost as if I did no selling at all – rather, I made it easier for the customer to buy! I now regularly present courses for this organization.

Mapping as a team activity

Mapping a conflict with all parties present is a powerful conflict resolution tool. It is best conducted with an independent and experienced facilitator. Since the main conflict protagonists are present, each one can be asked for their own needs and concerns in turn. The benefit of this type of mapping is a clear map, agreed by everyone present. What is more, the process itself of asking each person for their needs and concerns can very often promote a resolution of the conflict as this may be the first time the parties have had the opportunity to discuss the matter openly.

Mapping as a mediation tool

Some mediators like to use mapping as an additional visual representation of the mediation process.

Mapping involves the following steps:

1. Defining the issue.
2. Identifying all the stakeholders.
3. Listing stakeholders' needs and concerns.
4. Reading the map.
5. Brainstorming solutions.
6. Evaluating the alternatives.
7. Designing options.
8. Implementing the solution.
9. Seeking feedback and monitoring the results.

To illustrate this, we will now create a map of a conflict, using a case study as an example.

Case study: the new manager

In a private home for retired people, a new manager has been appointed to replace the previous incumbent who has just retired. The final decision to appoint this person was made by an outside firm of consultants in conjunction with the board of directors.

At the time the job became vacant, the assistant manager, Jean, had applied for the position. She had worked in the home for five years and was very competent at her job as well as being popular with the staff. Although she had no formal management qualifications, she had a natural empathetic style with staff and residents, and understood all the links needed with the local authorities and suppliers, both at a formal and informal level.

The new manager, Shirley, has a management degree and an excellent track record in her previous jobs. Although they were all service based, she had never worked in private care before. She prides herself on her efficiency and her ability to make sure the job is done. However, she upset the staff right from the start and disrupted the atmosphere by introducing new systems and procedures, which are still in the teething-problems stage. She demanded a level of punctuality, efficiency and discipline in the office that the staff had never experienced before, and they resent it. The resentment is being fuelled by Jean, who disliked Shirley from the start and is even more entrenched in her opposition now. Shirley, who is aware of the situation and the reasons behind Jean's resentment, is determined to get on with the job and hopes to win Jean over at some point. She does not want to lose her as Jean is so well liked and so reliable.

The residents, meanwhile, have noticed the change in ambience and the pointed digs some of the staff members make about Shirley. Their natural inclination is to side with Jean with whom they have dealt over the years. On the other hand, they have no complaints about Shirley and some of the new procedures she has introduced have benefited them greatly. They can already see an improvement in their daily schedules, which are far less regimented, and they actually look forward to their meals now!

One morning, the problem 'boils over'. Shirley overruled a decision made by Jean without referring to her. Jean has had enough. She walks into Shirley's office and the result is a loud and bitter exchange of words between them. The staff and residents are affected, and one of the older residents is in tears as she simply cannot cope with noise and shouting. Shirley decides that she may need outside help in dealing with the situation, however, she decides to give it one last go. She asks Jean to a meeting to try and resolve the situation.

They decide to use mapping as a tool to help their discussion (for further details see Hollier, Murray, and Cornelius, 1993).

Defining the issue

On a large flipchart or whiteboard, Shirley and Jean need to find a broad label for the problem and circle it. The label should not include any named persons and should be defined as objectively as possible. Supposing you were to ask each of the four main parties involved for their definition of the issue in question, we might receive the following responses:

- Jean would say 'The problem with Shirley'.
- Shirley would say 'Jean's resentment'.
- The residents would say 'The atmosphere in the residential home'.
- The staff would say 'Deteriorating morale'.

Jean and Shirley need to agree a neutral phrase summing up the problem. They could use 'Better relationships at work' or 'Our future together' or 'Office morale'. Test the label to make sure it does not contain presuppositions, judgements or solutions. Sometimes the label chosen is not the right one and as you start working on the map, you will suddenly find the issue has become clearer and you will want to change the label. The main aim is to have a label on the flipchart with which all present can identify. We will choose 'Office morale'.

Identifying all the stakeholders

The main protagonists are obvious stakeholders. Who else might be or become involved in this situation, either currently or if the problem worsened? Other staff, residents, board of directors, outside consultants, local authorities etc.?

The trick to completing the stakeholders' list is to obtain as broad a picture as you can. For example, you may need to add as stakeholders the partners of the protagonists, as loss of a job could influence them. You may need to subdivide and name particularly important customers or suppliers. On one occasion, I recall mapping an issue that involved relocation. One of the stakeholders was a cat! As one of those involved in the move, her needs and concerns had to be taken into account.

Very often we start examining the issue without realizing that there could be repercussions or side effects elsewhere. We concentrate so closely on the parties involved that we forget the impact the problem or the solution could have on other departments or other parts of our lives.

Celia, a participant on one of my mapping workshops, reported that she had used this technique to help her resolve a tricky issue. She had to make one of two people redundant. They had both joined on the same day so they could not use the 'last in, first out' rule of thumb. They were both women. They were roughly the same age. They were both equally competent at the job and equally loyal to the company and popular with colleagues. Celia had an almost impossible choice and at times wished she could volunteer for redundancy herself and save both their jobs.

In the end, by mapping the situation and extending the stakeholder's list beyond that of the obvious, Celia noticed that one of the two employees had no dependants, while the other had an elderly disabled mother to look after. This stimulated the thought that perhaps the carer would welcome working part-time. This, in turn, gave her the thought that she could offer them both a job-sharing opportunity, thus widening her options beyond the either/or situation she had been in. As often happens when we widen our options, Celia set off a favourable chain of events. One of the two employees, given the choice of a job share or redundancy, willingly took redundancy. Mapping moves in mysterious ways.

It is often useful to have another section for 'Others'; however, if new stakeholders emerge as you proceed, just draw another line and add them to the map. Try to keep the spaces even so that you give each person equal room to write their needs and concerns. You may group individuals if their needs and concerns are shared, and you may include groups and individuals on the same map, if you wish.

Listing stakeholders' needs and concerns

Now in each section write the words 'Needs' and 'Concerns'. You may wish to use different coloured markers for the headings and write them down in pencil in smaller writing to make sure it all fits.

1. Needs. We have already examined the issue of needs and concerns earlier on. We can loosely identify needs as what you want, or your angle or 'What's your interest in the problem?' Ask each stakeholder in turn for their main needs and write them down. Refer to Chapter 4 to refresh your memory on how to elicit needs. Sometimes a person may feel uncomfortable revealing their true needs. They could regard it as showing a soft underbelly or becoming vulnerable. If you feel

that anyone is showing excessive discomfort (some discomfort may be inevitable), then just go with the need they offer you for now and see if the issue can be reopened when reading the map.

2. Concerns. Ask each stakeholder if he or she has any concerns. Make sure concerns are not just the flipside of needs. If a concern can be worded positively, do so and list it under needs. For example, 'Not being included in the weekly planning meetings' could be reworded as a need 'to be included in the weekly planning meetings'. Once it is reworded as a need, test it as before to make sure it is a need and not a solution. With the above example, perhaps the need is to be kept abreast of events, in which case receiving the minutes of the meeting could be a feasible alternative. Bear in mind that it is sometimes easier for a person to list their concerns than to disclose their needs. Make good use of your empathy and listening skills to recognize needs and concerns.

Sometimes charting one person's needs and concerns prompts another person present to start talking about his/her own needs. It is paramount to keep both empathy and focus going. Write down one of their needs in their section and ask them if it is in order to go back to the other person and complete that before continuing with his or hers. That way you save face and maintain the core focus.

When listing needs and concerns, people are often diverted into recalling anecdotes or events, discussing their emotions, offering solutions, diagnosing motives, and so on. As a facilitator, you do need to keep everyone gently on track. Here are some questions you may find useful to ask if people are digressing:

- How is this relevant to your need/concern?
- If so and so were here, would he or she agree that was a need/concern?
- So if you got that, what else would it resolve?
- What would happen if this concern were realized?
- What would it take for all of these needs to be fulfilled?
- Supposing you could not get (your need), what else would satisfy you?
- I am wondering if that is a solution? What is the underlying need there?

Remember that the process of eliciting everyone's needs and concerns may throw up a solution before you have finished the

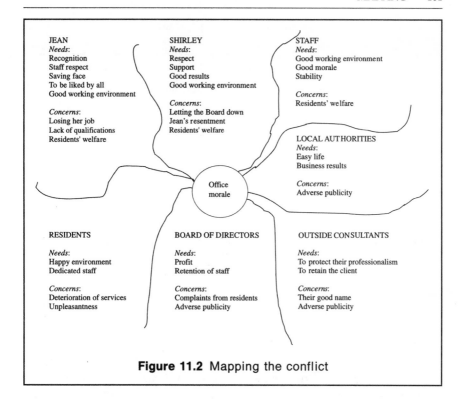

Figure 11.2 Mapping the conflict

process. Do not be tempted to stop at that point. Remember that a solution is exactly that – *a* solution, not necessarily *the* solution. What you require are options – jumping to an immediate solution blocks creativity. You need to complete the process before you can even begin to design your options and select appropriate solutions.

Your finished map will look like Figure 11.2.

Reading your map

When you are all satisfied that the map has been completed, and is an accurate reflection of what has been said by all parties (or what you imagine other parties would say if they were present), then and only then should you begin to read the map.

The purpose of the stakeholder map is not to offer solutions, although some may become apparent as you begin to read it. Rather it is to make the situation clearer, to see the 'whole elephant' and to see the relationship between parts (see Table 11.1).

We could reflect on the following concerns.

Table 11.1 Reading the map

Notice	Ask:
Shared needs and concerns	Can we find any common ground among the stakeholders?
Unique needs and concerns	Do any of the stakeholders have a particular or different angle?
Hidden needs and concerns	Are any declared needs masking: * deeper needs and concerns? * hidden agendas?
New angles or intuitions	What are we seeing now that we did not see before?
Leads or clues	What particularly difficult areas require extra attention? What have you noticed that is worth following up or finding more information about?

1. All those working in the home are concerned with residents' welfare. All need a good working environment. Jean needs recognition and the respect of the staff working for her. She also is concerned with saving face. Shirley is concerned with good business results and with not letting the board down. The outside authorities are concerned with the good name of the residential home and to ensure no adverse publicity. The residents want continuing good service and to have a happy environment.
2. We may also wonder if Jean and Shirley are clashing because of different behavioural styles. Perhaps we wonder if Jean is more of a people contemplative person while Shirley is more task expressive. This could give us another clue as to why they have not been able to communicate effectively from the start.
3. We may wonder if Shirley could have avoided much of the unpleasantness by taking time to talk to Jean right at the start, using some of the assertiveness skills we learnt, such as 'I' statements. That may lead you to thinking that Jean could use some management skills training to boost her confidence and enable her to apply for another job.

There are probably many more issues which you will have begun to notice or for which you need more detailed information. This is the purpose of the mapping session. It produces a visual aid to enable you to proceed to the next step.

Brainstorming solutions

To understand the rules of brainstorming, we need to remember the separate functions of the left and right hemispheres of the brain. To brainstorm creatively, we need to encourage our right brain to think freely. This very often entails breaking a pattern of left-brain thinking. We tend to use our logical, vertical, left-brain thinking even when a more creative, lateral, right-brain thinking technique is required.

Albert Einstein is quoted as saying 'The significant problems we face cannot be resolved by the same level of thinking that created them'. It is interesting to reflect how we often try to use left-brain thinking to solve problems that were created by the left brain in the first place. If we switch to right-brain thinking, we can often find a solution more readily.

For one of the most user-friendly explanations of right- and left-brain thinking, I recommend Betty Edwards (1979) *Drawing on the Right Side of the Brain*. I have found this book to be an invaluable aid to bringing out our latent creativity. Often, our left-brain thinking is dominant and by encouraging our right-brain thinking, we increase our thinking abilities overall. In this case, one and one make much more than two.

These are the strategies that I have found most useful in stimulating the right brain to come up with ideas:

- Use a large sheet of paper and many different coloured marker pens.
- Have one person as scribe.
- Write down the issue in the middle of the paper and circle it as you did for the mapping exercise.
- Give yourself a time limit, say, ten minutes. You will soon get a feel for how much time will be required. The larger the group the longer the time needed.
- Welcome outrageous and hugely silly ideas. Encourage laughter and free flow of thinking.
- All ideas, no matter how outrageous or impractical, are recorded without evaluation, judgement, criticism or comment. Write them down using exactly the same words in which they were expressed. Edited or modified versions of the idea are not the same.
- Ideas are not written in list form or sequentially. To encou-

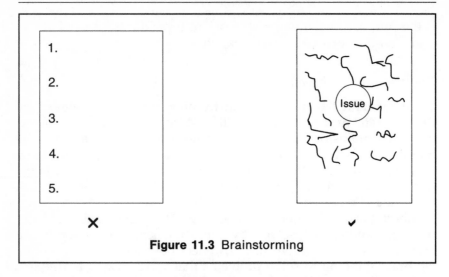

Figure 11.3 Brainstorming

rage the right hemisphere to be at its most creative, ideas should be recorded randomly all over the paper (Figure 11.3).

By encouraging the free flow of right-brain thinking, we can collect lots of ideas. Some of these may seem silly at first but they may prove to be the basis for a very good idea or they may just trigger off another idea either in the same person or another. Being provocative might just spark off other thoughts.

For example, in one brainstorming session, about a department that required absolute quiet in which to accomplish their work, one participant suggested that the department should be housed in a rocket and sent to outer space. This led to the idea of rehousing the department in the annex across the yard used for storing old files and moving the files into the space currently occupied by the department in question.

Some brainstorming ideas for the case study:

- Send Jean on a management training course.
- Send Shirley on a people skills course.
- Put Jean and Shirley on different shifts.
- Split the responsibilities.
- Bring in an external mediator.

And some outrageous ideas:

- Fire both Jean and Shirley.
- Jean and Shirley to take it in turns to manage the residential home.

- Create self-managing home with the residents elected to a committee.

Evaluating the alternatives

We now need to bring an element of left-hemisphere thinking into the process. Out of this wealth of creative ideas, how can we begin to evaluate our options?

First, what are your criteria for judging which ideas will be most appropriate? Write down about five or six criteria. This is one time when you can start the sentence with a 'should', for example:

The suggestion should:

- meet the most needs
- cost no more than £xx to implement
- be fair to all concerned
- be on a try and see basis
- be a long-term solution.

Now think back to the ideas on the sheet and group those that seem to go together or to be linked in some way. This way, you will end up with a smaller number of groups, for each of which you can write a heading. Give each idea a score according to how well they meet the agreed criterion.

The most popular solution was to enable Jean to acquire qualifications and to study for an NVQ in management skills. This would increase her confidence and enable her to seek promotion. Certainly it would increase her chances of securing the job should Shirley move on.

Designing options

By now you will have a much clearer picture and some definite directions and solutions to move towards. Making the final decision depends on the task, the people and the organization concerned. Some points to consider are:

- task: complexity, constraints, consequences
- people: time, expertise, expectations, needs, beliefs
- organization: culture, resources, values, structure, style.

Occasionally, a solution may have to be 'chunked down' into manageable tasks, or considered over the longer term.

Implementing the solution

How many precious management hours have you spent in meetings, analysing problems, suggesting solutions and then watching them being swallowed into a bureaucratic vortex? In many companies, the art of procrastination reigns supreme and many a brilliant idea is out of date by the time it is stamped with the approval of authority.

At an organizational level, this often indicates a lack of trust and communication. In other words, the powers that be may have instructed their line managers to examine the problem, produce a solution and then present their findings for approval. The approval process takes forever, the problem continues to deteriorate, everyone gets demoralized and a few weeks or months down the line, a crisis erupts.

If you and/or your organization are serious about implementing new ideas to resolve conflict, then you need to draw up an action plan and assign clear tasks to particular people and time limits for implementation.

Seeking feedback and monitoring the results

When an action plan has been agreed by all those involved, in whatever manner this agreement has been sought, the next step is to allow a suitable time limit for monitoring and to arrange for a follow-up meeting to review the results. All those involved in the initial mapping session should attend the review. This is an important step. So often, a 'solution' is found and the parties involved are left to get on with it. With no feedback, no support and no reviews, no wonder the problem sometimes does not go away!

When the issue is obscured

Sometimes, we know there is a conflict, we know something is wrong, but we are unable to pinpoint the reason. When this happens, it can be a good idea to use a cluster diagram to try and reach the heart of the matter. This process is best done on your own.

Exercise

Concentrate for a few moments on the conflict you are trying to resolve. Now write down on the middle of a sheet of paper the first thought that comes to mind and circle it. This thought could be an emotion such as 'Worried' or 'Upset' or a thought that crossed your mind such as 'Danger'. It could be a word or phrase that you have heard or used recently and which is playing on your mind such as 'You won't get far with that attitude of yours'. It could be an issue such as 'Sam and Liam's constant bickering' or 'Simon's moods'. Whatever it is that comes to mind at the time, write it down on the paper as it stands without any value judgements. Say you chose the word 'Worried'.

Write down, again without judgement or questioning, the immediate connecting thoughts that come to mind from that word or phrase, circling each one and connecting it with a line to the word that triggered off that particular thought. You may soon have a cluster diagram that looks like that in Figure 11.4.

The issue is slowly becoming clearer. We still have some way to go though.

The next step is to stop and reflect on what you have written so far. What are the key words? Where are the connections being made? What seem to be the most important keywords? Highlight them in some way. What connections seem to be most relevant? Darken the connections or double them in some way

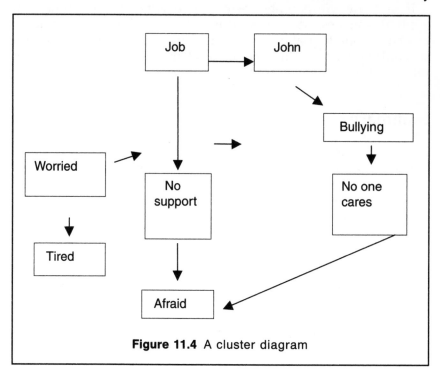

Figure 11.4 A cluster diagram

that makes sense to you. Do any symbols or pictures come to mind? Draw them in as well or allow yourself to doodle, if that is your inclination.

Now start asking yourself questions using the 'six bottoms on a fence' formula (see p. 73).

For example:

- Who is involved in this?
- What is it all about?
- How did it all start?
- When does it get worse?
- Where is it taking place?

Assessing the results

This process encourages you to consider a broad range of issues, which may previously have appeared unconnected. By allowing your right brain to grapple with the issue, you release many unconscious thoughts which should give you clear clues as to what is bothering you.

If you are disappointed with the results the first time you apply this process, do persist. It may take some time and practice to allow your thoughts to surface. However, the first time you succeed, you will realize the value of using cluster diagrams for thinking through your problems.

Summary

In this chapter we learnt the value and skill of creating a stakeholders' map to help us resolve conflicts. This is a skill that can be applied as a group or on our own. Then we examined some basic problem-solving techniques and issues that influence our decision-making. Finally, we examined the cluster diagram technique for clarifying obscure issues.

12

Mediation

It is unfortunate that the parties most directly involved in a dispute may be in the worst position to settle the dispute.

(Edward de Bono, author, and creator of lateral thinking)

Sometimes, conflicts worsen to the point where third party intervention is required. Knowing how to mediate in staff conflicts is a very useful management skill. This chapter does not purport to turn you into a fully qualified mediator, but it will give you a few basic processes and techniques to enable you to carry out a simple mediation process and help you keep the peace. Using these simple techniques could well prevent a conflict requiring a full industrial tribunal or a formal disciplinary session.

The *Pocket Oxford Dictionary* defines to mediate as 'intervene (between two persons or groups) for purpose of reconciling them'. The mediator helps the negotiating parties to come to their own agreement. He or she does not solve their problems for them. Mediation is the most informal of the conflict resolution methods involving a third party. Others include conciliation, arbitration and litigation.

Conciliation is concerned with reducing hostilities and finding some common working agreement. It does not necessarily include mediation.

Mediation UK (1995) define the differences between mediation and arbitration as follows:

1. *Mediation.* A process by which an impartial third party helps disputing parties work out an agreement. The disputants, not the mediator, decide the terms of this agreement. Mediation usually focuses on future rather than past behaviour.
2. *Arbitration.* A process in which an impartial third party makes a final, usually binding, decision. The discussion and decision, while structured, may not be as rigidly restricted by formal procedures and rules of evidence as is courtroom procedure.

Mediation is used widely in the USA and is gaining ground in the UK. Mediation UK is one of the foremost associations involved with promoting mediation in the UK and anyone interested in becoming a qualified mediator could contact them as a first step (see Appendix II).

What are some of the advantages of mediation?

- The negotiating parties agree on appointing the mediator, producing an element of common ground even before the process starts.
- The mediator helps the negotiating parties focus on the needs and concerns of each party.
- Skilled mediators have acquired a conflict-resolving mindset and commonly use a win/win approach.
- The negotiating parties have equal power at the negotiating table. No party has an advantage.
- The mediator's presence can often calm emotionally charged encounters.
- There is often more commitment to implementing the solution because the negotiating parties were in control of the content throughout.

What are the skills and qualities of a mediator?

Imagine that you were in conflict with another party and you had both agreed to the issue being referred to a mediator. What qualities and skills would the ideal candidate possess?

Qualities

1. Impartiality and fairness. This is often cited as the main requirement; being neutral and not favouring one side over the other.
2. A genuine and sympathetic understanding of how people behave. This implies experience with a wide variety of people and in many different situations; a basic knowledge of people.
3. Analysis skills. The ability to analyse the situation objectively and to assess the chances of agreements and commitments.
4. Understanding the issue to be resolved. A basic knowledge of the rules and regulations, systems and procedures involved in particular issues – for example, employment legislation or company codes of conduct may prohibit certain solutions from being implemented.
5. Self-awareness and continuous personal development. The ability to reflect and learn from mistakes and experiences. An understanding of one's own strengths and weaknesses.
6. Openness and commitment to equality. This means being aware of personal prejudices and projections. It also means being dedicated to equal opportunities and dealing with people without any discrimination.
7. Integrity. Mediators should be honest, decent, law-abiding and principled. They should be seen to live up to their declared codes of ethics.
8. Flexibility and creativity. The ability to notice when a process is not working and to try another; the ability to think laterally and offer different ideas.
9. Balance. The ability to see things from different viewpoints and to balance one's own feelings and prejudices with the requirements of the mediation in hand; the ability to balance authority and control with respect and empathy.
10. Professionalism. The ability to demonstrate a professional image at all times. This includes attention to hygiene and appearance, being punctual and genuinely committed to the job in hand.

The skills of a mediator

The skills we have covered in this book form the basis of mediation training:

- recognizing levels of conflict
- eliciting needs and concerns

- choosing response over reaction
- creating empathy
- listening and communication skills
- appropriate assertiveness
- recognizing power issues
- coping with emotions (own and others)
- mapping and problem-solving.

The above skills on their own, important as they are, will not be enough to conduct a mediation session. We need to understand and be able to manage the mediation process throughout. Facilitation and presentation skills are also vital.

When is mediation appropriate in the workplace?

Mediation is ideally suited to workplace disputes. I have observed numerous cases of industrial disputes and formal disciplinary hearings that could have been avoided had a mediator been involved at an early enough stage. Continuing disputes and those taken to litigation also cause tension and low morale in the workplace. If all employees had conflict resolution training, fewer conflicts would reach crisis stage. And if each organization had one or two members of staff trained in mediation skills, or had access to experienced external mediators, fewer conflicts would be allowed to reach litigation.

Mediation should be considered when:

- good relationships must be maintained
- there is a breakdown in communication between the negotiating parties
- the conflicting parties do not have the necessary skills to resolve the matter on their own
- the negotiating parties do not trust each other
- the parties need to be made aware of external considerations
- both sides have a good case
- the balance of power is equal
- speed and discretion are important
- the parties wish to retain control of the outcome, ruling out arbitration and litigation.

Take a few moments to recall some conflicts of which you are aware that resulted in litigation, resignation, sacking or had some other lasting effect. With hindsight, you can probably see the levels of conflict, as described in Chapter 2, and how an early intervention could have avoided the crisis.

The mediation process

Individual mediators practise different forms of intervention and follow different theories. Some mediators use an evaluative and interest-based approach, as set out below, while others prefer a facilitative and transformational one. The purpose of this short introduction is to help you understand a simple and basic process that you should be able to use safely and effectively. Some useful resources are listed in Appendix II, in case you wish to explore this area further.

There are four phases in the mediation process, as shown in Figure 12.1.

Phase 1: preparation

The mediator meets each party separately. This meeting involves introductions, explaining the process and benefits of mediation and finding out the parties' issues. Start by inviting the parties to tell you what the problem is from their point of view. For example, 'In order for me to understand the problem, I would like you to describe what is happening right now'. Your active

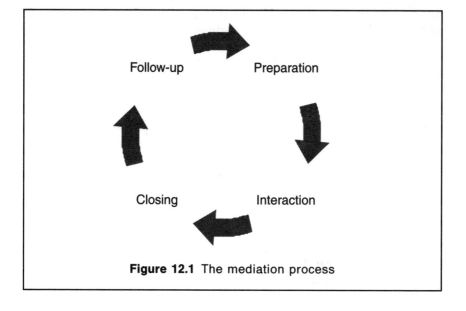

Figure 12.1 The mediation process

listening skills will serve you well here. Do not interrupt, minimize or reassure. It will aid the process if you allow the parties to air all their concerns.

It is very useful to establish what contingency plan the negotiating parties have in the event that the negotiation breaks down (Fisher and Ury, 1981). Ask 'What is the best you can hope for if you can't negotiate an agreement and what is the worst that can happen?'

Assume that the negotiating parties have a frosty relationship. At present, they survive by avoiding each other as much as possible. It prevents them coming to blows but does nothing to improve working relationships or morale in the office. Maintaining that frosty relationship may be their best alternative to a negotiated agreement. That is the position that they wish to improve. Now what is the worst that could happen? It could be that they inadvertently make things worse, involve other people or resurrect old issues. Their situation at work becomes untenable, and either party may feel they have no option but to resign.

Once this concept is explained, you need to move on to seeking agreement to the mediation process. Remember how important it is to ensure that both parties agree to attend voluntarily. Coercion is counter-productive. During the meeting, establish trust, impartiality and confidentiality.

The next stage involves the mediator examining the issues and deciding on the next course of action. For example, you may feel that you are not the ideal person to carry out the process. If you decide to go ahead, then the negotiating parties should be contacted, their commitment obtained and the venue decided.

Now you can turn to managing the environment. Where you meet is an important element of the process. The room needs to be quiet, comfortable and private. This means absolutely no interruptions, telephones, or people coming in. It should be on neutral ground to assist impartiality and ensure that neither one has a psychological advantage. Be aware of power issues in furniture and ensure that the three (or more) chairs are 'equal power' chairs. They should all be the same height and the same design, i.e. level of padding and armrests.

Whether a table is used or not is a matter of personal preference. Some people feel 'safer' with a table to rest on. I myself prefer a round table for mediations so that the negotiating parties are not face to face. However, it is up to the mediator to ensure that he or she is seated in the middle, equidistant from both parties to convey strict impartiality. The smallest details count.

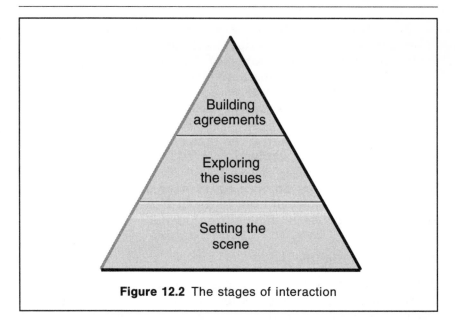

Figure 12.2 The stages of interaction

Phase 2: interaction

There are three distinct stages to the interaction (see Figure 12.2).

Stage 1: setting the scene

There are three main tasks.

1. *Make the parties feel welcome,* comfortable and at ease in what might be a highly fraught and possibly tense situation. The parties are likely to be nervous and apprehensive. Carry out the personal introductions and establish how each party wishes to be addressed. Explain the purposes of the mediation and the role of the mediator as previously explored.
2. *Establish ground rules.* It is useful to have these on a flipchart that is prominently displayed, or you could have them typed out in advance and given to each party.
3. *Establish and seek agreement for ground rules.* Allow the parties to add their own rules, if appropriate, and if all can agree to them. The following are the basic minimum to observe:
   a) Each party will have an equal amount of time to explain their case.
   b) Only one party can speak at a time, while the other listens.
   c) All present should maintain open, honest, and tactful, communication.

d) No blaming, name calling or abusive language.
e) Everyone to remain seated at all times.
f) All parties will maintain confidentiality
g) The mediator has the authority to break or halt proceedings if rules are broken.
h) How long the session will last and what breaks are appropriate.
i) What will happen if no agreement has been reached during the time allocated.

There may be others appropriate to your own mediation. This part of the process should not be rushed. A successful outcome often depends on establishing a firm foundation.

Stage 2: exploring the issues

Now it is the turn of the negotiating parties to make their statements. Ensure they actively listen, as they will restate the other party's key points prior to continuing. For example:

> *Paul*: I'm absolutely fed up with John's continued interference with the way I do my job. He's on my back the whole time and constantly criticizes me.
> *Mediator*: John, could I hear you repeat back what Paul said?
> *John*: He says he's fed up with me interfering with the way he does his job and that I constantly criticize him.
> *Mediator*: Paul, are you satisfied that's what you said?
> *Paul*: Yes.

The mediator can now move on. However, if Paul said 'No, that's not what I said' the mediator repeats the process until the speaker is satisfied that he has been heard.

The mediator's role in this stage is to:

1. Recognize key needs and concerns: 'So, what is really bothering you is the apparent lack of cooperation', 'Do I understand correctly the key issue for you is fairness?'
2. Recognize common ground: 'This appears to be affecting you both', 'It seems to me you both want to do what is best'.
3. Check understanding: 'So, you have tried to make time, is that what you're saying?' 'Could you be more specific?'
4. Clarify assumptions: 'When you say there's no point, does

that mean you want to stop trying?' 'When you say taking you for granted, what does that mean to you?'

5. Accept differences and use normalizing statements to move on: 'Yes, it's never easy to make such adjustments', 'I understand that. It's a difficult time for you both.'
6. Acknowledge feelings and thank people for openly expressing them: 'I can see that is upsetting you and I appreciate you telling us.'
7. Maintain a balanced and safe environment: 'It's fine to express how you feel here, we've agreed nothing goes outside these four walls.'
8. Change the focus from the past to the future: 'I can really understand how difficult that must have been, what would it take to improve the situation?' 'That must have been frustrating, how can we make sure it doesn't happen again?'
9. Summarize and reflect: 'Let me make sure I understand the situation.' (State the situation objectively and briefly.) 'Is that what you're both saying?'
10. Obtain consensus before moving on: 'So, you both agree that overtime is an issue', 'Let me check what we have agreed on so far.'
11. Reinforce willingness to resolve when people show it: 'Thank you for suggesting that, Tim. Chris, how does that improve the situation?' 'Tim, Chris is prepared to give it a try. What about you?'

The question of note taking often arises. Should the mediator take notes or not? In the interests of confidentiality, it is often recommended that any notes taken, other than those detailing agreements, should be destroyed at the end of the mediation session. Note taking can often be distracting and disturbing for negotiating parties. If the mediator has to take notes, they should be written as unobtrusively as possible. My own preference is simply to write down a few key words, ensuring that I do not lose eye contact and rapport with the negotiating parties.

Stage 3: building agreements

This stage is reached only after everyone has had their say and the mediator moves the process towards finding options and mutually acceptable solutions. It is up to the mediator to encourage the parties to find their own solutions. A good question to ask is 'What would it take for the situation to improve?' or ask them to 'describe your ideal situation'.

The key tasks in this stage are to:

1. Recognize the areas of agreement.
2. Keep the parties focused on solutions, not problems.
3. Highlight every conciliatory gesture or statement made.
4. Reinforce common ground.
5. Develop options.
6. Evaluate the options.
7. Check agreements with each party.
8. Obtain commitment.

Occasionally, the need to talk to the negotiating parties individually may arise again, for example, if emotions run high or a need arises to clarify misunderstandings or misperceptions. This is sometimes known as caucusing. Establish with each party what issues may or may not be brought back to the negotiating table. When face-to-face mediation recommences, you will find it useful to re-establish trust and emphasize areas of agreement.

Phase 3: closing

In this stage, your main tasks are to check that the negotiating parties are fully committed to implementing the agreed solutions and agreeing a date for a meeting in which to follow up and debrief.

It is useful to put the agreements in writing and to give a copy to each party, retaining a copy for your files. The agreement should state the date and venue for the follow-up meeting.

Thank the negotiating parties for their cooperation and acknowledge their time, effort and willingness to resolve.

Phase 4: follow-up

The follow-up meeting should take between one and four weeks after the mediation process. The length of time given will depend on the amount of contact the parties are likely to have in the intervening period. If they are in daily contact, then a meeting arranged one week later is about right. If they have less contact, say they work in different locations, then a delay of three to four weeks would enable them to assess how the agreement is working out.

The venue for the follow-up meeting should be chosen with

the same care as the initial venue and the purpose of the meeting will be to check:

- the agreement is holding out
- the solution is workable
- whether minor adjustments need to be made
- how the relationships are going
- what future support they will require
- what warning signals will they pay attention to in future
- accepting responsibility for monitoring the situation on a continuing basis
- what steps should be taken if the agreement breaks down
- any other issues arising.

Some professional mediators have expressed concern that an untrained person should attempt to mediate, seeing it as a do-it-yourself job that could be botched up. I acknowledge their concern and would always recommend using a professional workplace mediator in complicated cases.

However, there are some simple cases where mediation is possible and could prevent a conflict from worsening. If the steps outlined above are rigorously adhered to, and the mediator has good conflict resolution and negotiation skills, then I have no hesitation in encouraging people to mediate. The more experience gained in simple mediations, the more skilful the person will become. I do not believe that there is such a mystique about the whole process – it is not rocket science.

We often pay so much attention to the negotiating parties and the mediation process that the mediator's own well-being is overlooked. Never forget that mediation can be a very stressful process. A good mediator in an office can sometimes find him or herself in great demand. If this is the case, then the mediator needs to find a good mentor or support network in order to debrief and receive feedback.

It is always useful for a mediator to build in a period of reflection after the mediation process. This helps keep the mediator on task and is part of the continuing professional development process.

Summary

In this chapter, we examined the process of mediation and the skills and qualities required of a mediator. We suggested conflicts that were suitable for mediation purposes. Then we moved on to the mediation process itself. We examined the preparation stages, prior to the encounter and the face-to-face encounter. Finally, we considered the debrief and follow-up, and the support required for both the mediator and the negotiating parties.

Appendix I:
References and bibliography

Acland A. F. (1990), *A Sudden Outbreak of Common Sense*, London: Hutchinson Business Books.

Aristotle (1998), *The Nichomachean Ethics*, trans D. Ross, J. R. Ackrill and J. O. Urmson, Oxford: Oxford Paperbacks.

Arnold, J., Robertson, I. T. and Cooper, C. L. (1991), *Work Psychology: Understanding Human Behaviour in the Workplace*, London: Pitman.

Berne, E. (1964), *Games People Play*, New York: Grove Press.

Bolton, R. (1979), *People Skills*, London: Simon and Schuster.

de Bono, E. (1977), *Lateral Thinking*, London: Pelican.

de Bono, E. (1985), *Conflicts: A Better Way to Resolve Them*, Harmondsworth: Penguin.

Boring, E. G. (1930), (Article title not available), *American Journal of Psychology*, **42**, 444–5.

Cassell Concise English Dictionary (1989), B. Kirkpatrick (ed.), thumb-indexed edn, London: Cassell.

Charvet, S. R. (1997), *Words that Change Minds*, Dubuque, IA: Kendall Hunt.

Cooper C., Cooper, R. D. and Eaker, L. H. (1988), *Living with Stress*, Harmondsworth: Penguin.

Cooper, R. and Sawaf, A. (1997), *Executive EQ*, London: Orion Publishing.

Cornelius H. and Faire, S. (1989), *Everyone Can Win*, East Rosevill, NSW: Simon and Schuster.

Cornelius H., Murray, K., Spencer, R., Faire, S. and Hall, S. (1992), *Conflict Resolution Skills for the School Community: Inservice Trainers Manual Edition 2*, Chatswood, NSW: Conflict Resolution Network.

Crainer, S. (1997), *The Ultimate Business Quotations*, Oxford: Capstone.

Crawley, J. (1992), *Constructive Conflict Management*, London: Nicholas Brealey.

Crum, T. (1987), *The Magic of Conflict*, New York: Simon and Schuster, USA.

Daniel, D. Mediation Training Institute International, web site at http://www.mediationworks.com/mti/

Dilts, R. (1990), *Changing Belief Systems with NLP*, Cupertino: Meta Publications.

Edwards, B. (1979), *Drawing on the Right Side of the Brain*, London: HarperCollins (paperback edition 1993).

Fischer, L. (1962), *The Essential Gandhi*, New York: Vintage.

Fisher, R. and Ury, W. (1981), *Getting To Yes*, London: Arrow Books.

Fisher, R., Kopelman, E. and Schneider, A. K. (1994), *Beyond Machiavelli*, Harmondsworth: Penguin.

French, J. and Raven, B. (1958), The Bases of Social Power, in D. Cartwright (ed.) *Studies in Social Power*, Ann Arbor, MI: Institute for Social Research.

Goleman, D. (1995), *Emotional Intelligence*, London: Bloomsbury.

Gray, J. (1993), *Men Are from Mars, Women Are from Venus*, London: Thorsons.

Handy, C. (1976), *Understanding Organisations*, Harmondsworth: Penguin.

Handy, C. (1978), *Gods of Management*, London: Business Books.

Hanson, P. (1986), *The Joy of Stress*, London: Pan Books.

Harris, T. A. (1973), *I'm OK – You're OK*, London: Pan.

Hollier, F., Murray, K. and Cornelius, H. (1993), *The Conflict Resolution Trainers' Manual: 12 Skills*. Chatswood, NSW: Conflict Resolution Network.

Honey, P. and Mumford, A. (1992), *The Manual of Learning Styles*, 3rd edn, UK: Honey.

Hopson, B., Scally, M. and Stafford, K. (1992), *Transitions: The Challenge of Change*, London: Mercury Business.

Health and Safety Executive (HSE) (1995), *Stress At Work: A Guide for Employers*, London: HSE Books.

Institute of Personnel and Development (IPD) (1998), *Key Facts on Stress*, London: IPD.

Jeffers, S. (1987), *Feel the Fear and Do It Anyway*. London: Arrow Books.

Johns, C. (1995), Framing Learning through Reflection Within, in *Carper's Fundamental Ways of Knowing in Nursing*, London: Blackwell Science.

Kroger, W. S. (1963), *Clinical and Experimental Hypnosis*, Philadelphia: J. B. Lippincott.

Laborde, G. (1987), *Influencing with Integrity*, Palo Alto, CA: Syntony.

Lao-Tzu (1988), *Tao Te Ching*, trans. S. Mitchell, London: Kyle Cathie.

Lindenfield, G. (1993), *Managing Anger*, London: Thorsons.

Looker, T. and Gregson, O. (1989), *Stresswise*, London: Hodder and Stoughton.

Mallinger, A. E. and de Wyze, J. (1993), *Too Perfect*, London: Thorsons.

Maltz, M. (1960), *Psycho-Cybernetics*, London: Pocket Books.

McDermott, I. and O'Connor, J. (1996), *Practical NLP For Managers*, Aldershot: Gower.

Mediation UK (1995), *Training Manual in Community Mediation Skills*, ref. S2-55, May, Bristol: Mediation UK.

Mehrabian, A. (1971), *Silent Messages*, Belmont, CA: Wadsworth. (For further information on Professor Mehrabian's work, visit his web site on www.kaaj.com/psych/home.html)

Morgan, G. (1986) *Images of Organisation* (2nd edn, 1997), London: Sage.

O'Connor, J. and Seymour, J. (1993), *Introducing NLP* (revd edn), London: Acquarian Press.

Parslow, E. (1992), *Coaching, Assessing and Mentoring*, London: Kogan Page.

Randall, P. (1997), *Adult Bullying*, London: Routledge.

Robbins, A. (1992), *Awaken the Giant Within*, London: Simon and Schuster.

Schafer, W. (1987), *Stress Management for Wellness*, Orlando, FL: Holt, Rinehart and Winston.

Shaw, G. B. (1988), *Man and Superman*, Harmondsworth: Penguin.

Stott, K. and Walker, A. (1992), *Making Management Work*, Singapore: Simon and Schuster.

Tannen, D. (1990), *You Just Don't Understand*, New York: Ballantine Books.

Tannen, D. (1992), *That's Not What I Meant*, London: Virago Press.

The Pocket Oxford Dictionary (1984), (7th edn), Oxford: Oxford University Press.

Ury, W. (1991), *Getting Past No*, London: Century Business.

Whetten, D., Cameron, K. and Woods, M. (1996), *Effective Problem Solving*, London: HarperCollins.

Appendix II:
Sources and resources

Neuro-linguistic programming

1. The Association of Neuro-Linguistic Programming (ANLP) was formed in 1985 as a non-profit-making organization to serve as a focal point for all those interested in NLP. For further information contact:

   ANLP
   PO Box 10
   Porthmadog
   LL48 6ZB
   Tel: 01785 660665
   (Please include four first-class stamps for an information pack.)

2. The Anglo American bookshop has a first-class selection of books on NLP. You can request a catalogue from:

   The Anglo American Book Company Limited
   Crown Buildings
   Bancyfelin
   Carmarthen SA33 5ND
   Tel: 01267 211880 or 01267 211886
   Web site: http://www.anglo-american.co.uk

3. Many books on NLP are available from good bookshops. Here are some of my personal favourites:

Andreas, C. and Andreas, A. (1989), *Heart of the Mind*, Moab, UT: Real People Press.

Andreas, S. and Faulkner, C. (1996), *NLP: The New Technology of Achievement*, London: Nicholas Brealey.

Bandler, R. and Grinder, J. (1979), *Frogs into Princes*, Moab, UT: Real People Press.

Knight, S. (1995), *NLP at Work*, London: Nicholas Brealey.

McDermott, I. and O'Connor, J. (1996), *Practical NLP for Managers*, Aldershot: Gower.

O'Connor, J. and Seymour, J. (1993), *Introducing NLP*, London: Aquarian Press.

Conflict resolution and mediation

1. The Conflict Resolution Network is a network of people with a common commitment to conflict resolution, cooperative communication strategies and related skills. For further information contact:

    Conflict Resolution Network
    PO Box 1016
    Chatswood
    NSW 2057
    Australia
    Tel: (02) 9419 8500
    Fax: (02) 9413 1148
    Web site: crnhq.org

2. Conflict Resolution (UK) organize conflict resolution in-house training courses based on materials supplied by the Conflict Resolution Network of Australia. For further information contact:

    Conflict Resolution (UK)
    30 The Crossways
    Wembley Park
    Middlesex HA9 9NG
    Tel: 020 8904 2474
    Fax: 020 8904 7773

3. The Centre for Dispute Resolution (CEDR) is internationally recognized as providing expert third party conflict management and training including 'Mediation skills at work' – a

course which teaches those in management the skills of effective mediation in the workplace. For further information contact:

CEDR
Princes House
95 Gresham Street
London EC2V 7NA
Tel: 020 7645 1437
Fax: 020 7600 0500

4. Elizabeth Rivers offers training courses on conflict resolution using techniques from aikido and other non-aggressive martial arts, based on the work of Thomas Crum, author of *The Magic of Conflict* (Crum, 1987). For further information contact:

Elizabeth Rivers
Confluence Consultancy
24 Diana Road
London E17 5LF
Tel: 020 8527 8654
Fax: 020 8523 4549

5. Mediation UK is working to promote constructive ways of resolving conflicts and repairing damage caused in the community, and to ensure that everyone has access to quality mediation in their local communities.

Mediation UK
Alexander House
Telephone Avenue
Bristol BS1 4BS
Tel: 0117 904 6661
Fax: 0117 904 3331
E-mail: mediationuk@mediationuk.org.uk
Web site: http://www.mediationuk.org.uk

Index

The Gower Handbook of Management

Fourth Edition

Edited by Dennis Lock

'If you have only one management book on your shelf, this must be the one.'

Dennis Lock recalls launching the first edition in 1983 with this aim in mind. It has remained the guiding principle behind subsequent editions, and today *The Gower Handbook of Management* is widely regarded as a manager's bible: an authoritative, gimmick-free and practical guide to best practice in management. By covering the broadest possible range of subjects, this *Handbook* replicates in book form a forum in which managers can meet experts from a range of professional disciplines.

The new edition features:

• 65 expert contributors - many of them practising managers and all of them recognized authorities in their field
• many new contributors: over one-third are new to this edition
• 72 chapters, of which half are completely new
• 20 chapters on subjects new to this edition
• a brand new design and larger format.

The Gower Handbook of Management has received many plaudits during its distinguished career, summed up in the following review from *Director*:

'... packed with information which can be used either as a reference work on a specific problem or as a guide to an entire operation. In a short review one can touch only lightly on the richness and excellence of this book, which well deserves a place on any executive bookshelf.'

Gower

Gower Handbook of Management Skills

Third Edition

Edited by Dorothy M Stewart

'This is the book I wish I'd had in my desk drawer when I was first a manager. When you need the information, you'll find a chapter to help; no fancy models or useless theories. This is a practical book for real managers, aimed at helping you manage more effectively in the real world of business today. You'll find enough background information, but no overwhelming detail. This is material you can trust. It is tried and tested.'

So writes Dorothy Stewart, describing in the Preface the unifying theme behind the Third Edition of this bestselling *Handbook*. This puts at your disposal the expertise of 25 specialists, each a recognized authority in their particular field. Together, this adds up to an impressive 'one stop library' for the manager determined to make a mark.

Chapters are organized within three parts: Managing Yourself, Managing Other People, and Managing the Business. Part I deals with personal skills and includes chapters on self-development and information technology. Part II covers people skills such as listening, influencing and communication. Part III looks at finance, project management, decision-making, negotiating and creativity. A total of 12 chapters are completely new, and the rest have been rigorously updated to fully reflect the rapidly changing world in which we work.

Each chapter focuses on detailed practical guidance, and ends with a checklist of key points and suggestions for further reading.

Gower

Gower Handbook of Training and Development

Third Edition

Edited by Anthony Landale

It is now crystal clear that, in today's ever-changing world, an organization's very survival depends upon how it supports its people to learn and keep on learning. Of course this new imperative has considerable implications for trainers who are now playing an increasingly critical role in supporting individuals, teams and business management. In this respect today's trainers may need to be more than excellent presenters; they are also likely to require a range of consultancy and coaching skills, to understand the place of technology in supporting learning and be able to align personal development values with business objectives.

This brand new edition of the *Gower Handbook of Training and Development* will be an invaluable aid for today's training professional as they face up to the organizational challenges presented to them. All 38 chapters in this edition are new and many of the contributors, whilst being best-selling authors or established industry figures, are appearing for the first time in this form. Edited by Anthony Landale, this *Handbook* builds on the foundations that previous editions have laid down whilst, at the same time, highlighting many of the very latest advances in the industry.

The *Handbook* is divided into five sections - learning organization, best practice, advanced techniques in training and development, the use of IT in learning, and evaluation issues.

Gower